CHILDREN'S ISSUES, LAWS AND PROGRAMS

STATE CHILDREN'S HEALTH INSURANCE PROGRAM

EFFECTS ON COVERAGE AND SELECTED COSTS TO CONSUMERS

CHILDREN'S ISSUES, LAWS AND PROGRAMS

Additional books in this series can be found on Nova's website under the Series tab.

Additional e-books in this series can be found on Nova's website under the e-book tab.

CHILDREN'S ISSUES, LAWS AND PROGRAMS

STATE CHILDREN'S HEALTH INSURANCE PROGRAM

EFFECTS ON COVERAGE AND SELECTED COSTS TO CONSUMERS

TED WARNER
EDITOR

nova publishers
New York

Additional color graphics may be available in the e-book version of this book.

Library of Congress Cataloging-in-Publication Data

ISBN: 978-1-63483-673-9

Published by Nova Science Publishers, Inc. † New York

CONTENTS

PREFACE

CHIP is a joint federal-state program that finances health insurance for over 8 million children. Since the program's inception, the percentage of uninsured children nationwide has decreased by half, from 13.9 percent in 1997 to 6.6 percent in the first three months of 2014. This year, Congress will decide whether to extend CHIP funding beyond 2015. In this book, GAO examines what assessments of CHIP suggest about its effect on children's health care coverage and access; and what key issues identified by GAO's work the Congress may wish to consider in determining whether to extend CHIP funding.

In: State Children's Health Insurance Program ISBN: 978-1-63483-673-9
Editor: Ted Warner

Chapter 1

CHILDREN'S HEALTH INSURANCE PROGRAM: EFFECTS ON COVERAGE AND ACCESS, AND CONSIDERATIONS FOR EXTENDING FUNDING*

United States Government Accountability Office

ABBREVIATIONS

AHRQ	Agency for Healthcare Research and Quality
CAHPS	Consumer Assessment of Healthcare Providers and Systems
CARTS	Children's Health Insurance Program Annual Reporting Template System
CHIP	State Children's Health Insurance Program
CHIPRA	Children's Health Insurance Program Reauthorization Act of 2009
CMS	Centers for Medicare & Medicaid Services
CPS-ASEC	Current Population Survey Annual Social and Economic Supplement
EPSDT	Early and Periodic Screening, Diagnostic, and Treatment
FPL	federal poverty level

* This is an edited, reformatted and augmented version of The United States Government Accountability Office publication, GAO-15-348, dated February 2015.

HHS	Department of Health and Human Services
PPACA	Patient Protection and Affordable Care Act
QHP	Qualified Health Plan
SADP	stand-alone dental program

WHY GAO DID THIS STUDY

CHIP is a joint federal-state program that finances health insurance for over 8 million children. Since the program's inception, the percentage of uninsured children nationwide has decreased by half, from 13.9 percent in 1997 to 6.6 percent in the first three months of 2014. This year, Congress will decide whether to extend CHIP funding beyond 2015.

GAO was asked to provide information on the effect of CHIP on children's coverage, and what key issues may be considered in determining the ongoing need for CHIP. In this report, GAO examines (1) what assessments of CHIP suggest about its effect on children's health care coverage and access; and (2) what key issues identified by GAO's work the Congress may wish to consider in determining whether to extend CHIP funding.

For the assessments of CHIP's effect, GAO reviewed reports on CHIP, including a mandated evaluation and annual HHS reports on quality, which publish data that states report on Child Core Set measures, which are quality measures identified by HHS that states can use to monitor health care provided to children in CHIP and Medicaid. GAO also reviewed relevant federal statutes and regulations. To identify key issues that the Congress may wish to consider, GAO reviewed its own relevant reports and testimony; reviewed letters from state governors regarding CHIP; and interviewed CHIP officials in 10 states, which were selected based on variation in location, program size, and design.

HHS provided technical comments on a draft of this report, which GAO incorporated as appropriate.

WHAT GAO FOUND

Assessments of national data GAO reviewed identify positive effects of the State Children's Health Insurance Program (CHIP), and the quality measures reported by states help identify areas needing improvement.

- A mandated evaluation of CHIP published in 2014 noted that CHIP enrollees (1) had substantially better access to care, service use, and preventive care when compared with uninsured children; and (2) experienced comparable access and service use when compared with privately insured children. These findings are generally consistent with prior GAO work, which used national survey data to compare CHIP enrollees' access and service use with children who were uninsured or privately insured. When comparing CHIP enrollees with privately insured children, the mandated evaluation and prior GAO work differed regarding the utilization of certain services, such as emergency room use and dental services, which may be due to differences in when the data were collected and the particular measures that were used.
- The Department of Health and Human Services (HHS) also publishes data on quality measures that states voluntarily report annually. These Child Core Set measures show mixed results regarding service utilization among CHIP and Medicaid enrollees. For example, states reported that nearly all children aged 12 to 24 months enrolled in CHIP or Medicaid had at least one primary care physician visit during fiscal year 2013. However, states reported that far fewer children obtained dental prevention or treatment services, with a mean of 46 percent of children receiving a preventive dental service, and a mean of 25 percent receiving dental treatment services. HHS officials said that they use these data to help identify areas for improvement in the care provided in CHIP and Medicaid.

GAO's prior work has identified important issues related to cost, coverage, and access that Congress may wish to consider when determining the ongoing need for CHIP, many of which were similar to issues raised by officials from the 10 states GAO reviewed.

- With regard to cost, GAO's prior work found that costs—defined as deductibles, copayments, coinsurance, and premiums—were almost always less for selected CHIP plans when compared with states' benchmark health plans, which were the models for health plans available in health insurance exchanges established under the Patient Protection and Affordable Care Act. Officials in five states expressed concerns about the higher cost of exchange plans compared with CHIP and the implications for families' finances.

- With regard to coverage, GAO previously reported that selected CHIP and state benchmark plans were generally similar in terms of their coverage of selected services and the services on which they imposed limits. However, officials from several of the 10 states pointed out that for many services needed by children with special health care needs, CHIP coverage was more comprehensive than exchange plans.
- With regard to access, several states raised concerns about negative implications for children's coverage if CHIP funding is not reauthorized, including concerns that their states would lose gains made in covering children, who would also lose access to providers and dental care.

* * *

February 27, 2015

The Honorable Orrin G. Hatch
Chairman
Committee on Finance United States Senate

The Honorable Fred Upton
Chairman
Committee on Energy and Commerce
House of Representatives

The State Children's Health Insurance Program (CHIP), a joint federal-state program that was established by Congress in 1997, finances health insurance for over 8 million children whose household incomes are above the threshold for Medicaid eligibility. Prior to CHIP, private health insurance coverage for children had been declining every year since 1987—reaching its lowest level of about 66 percent of children in 1994. While Medicaid helped to cushion the effect of this decline, many of the children losing coverage were ineligible for Medicaid coverage.[1] Since the inception of CHIP, the percentage of uninsured children nationwide has decreased by half, from 13.9 percent in 1997 to 6.6 percent in the first 3 months of 2014.[2] The Centers for Medicare & Medicaid Services (CMS), within the Department of Health and Human Services (HHS), oversees CHIP, with states designing, managing, and administering the operations of their individual programs. States administer CHIP under broad federal requirements, and the programs vary, for example, in the services covered, costs to individuals and families, and eligibility requirements.[3]

Over the course of the program, Congress has enacted legislation at various times authorizing continued funding for CHIP. Most recently, the Patient Protection and Affordable Care Act (PPACA) appropriated federal CHIP funding through fiscal year 2015.[4] PPACA requires that beginning in October 2015, if a state's CHIP funding is insufficient to cover all CHIP-eligible children, the state must establish procedures to ensure that the children who are not covered by CHIP are screened for Medicaid.[5] If such children are determined to be ineligible for Medicaid, the children may be enrolled in a qualified health plan (QHP)—which are plans offered by private issuers through health insurance exchanges in that state—that has been certified as comparable to CHIP by the Secretary of HHS, if such a QHP is available.[6] Over the longer term, PPACA requires states to maintain eligibility levels for children in CHIP and Medicaid until fiscal year 2019. Thus, under current law, some states could choose to eliminate or scale back their programs beginning in fiscal year 2020, even if federal funds are available.

Given that the Congress will decide whether to extend CHIP funding beyond 2015, you asked us to provide information about the effect that CHIP has had on children's health care, and what key issues may be considered in determining the ongoing need for the CHIP program. In this report, we examine (1) what assessments of CHIP suggest about the effect of the program on children's health care coverage and access across states; and (2) what key issues the Congress may wish to consider in determining whether to extend CHIP funding.

To examine what assessments of CHIP suggest about the program's effect, we synthesized information from HHS reports on CHIP, including a mandated national evaluation on the evolution of the program (referred to as the mandated evaluation) and its role in providing health coverage to low-income children.[7] We also reviewed HHS's annual CHIP and Medicaid reports on quality for fiscal years 2011 through 2014, relying primarily on the 2014 report (referred to as the annual quality report), which use state-reported data to assess the quality of care provided to children enrolled in CHIP and Medicaid for the applicable fiscal year, and a series of issue briefs on state practices to improve the quality of care for children enrolled in these programs.[8] To obtain information on state CHIP reporting requirements and states' efforts to report data for the annual quality report, we reviewed federal statutes and regulations governing CHIP; and interviewed CHIP officials from 10 states, which were selected based on variation in states' CHIP program design, income eligibility level, program enrollment, and states' rate of uninsured children.[9] The 10 selected states were Alaska, Arizona, Indiana, Mississippi, Nevada, New Hampshire, Pennsylvania, Rhode Island, South Carolina, and Wisconsin. For the purposes of the annual quality report, states have the option to report CHIP and Medicaid data separately, but commonly report combined data for the two programs. We supplemented HHS's findings with relevant findings from our own issued reports, when applicable.

To identify key issues that the Congress may wish to consider in determining whether to extend funding for CHIP, we reviewed relevant reports and testimony that we issued from February 2009 through December 2014. In addition, we interviewed CHIP officials in selected states about considerations for the extension of CHIP funding, and reviewed letters from state governors regarding their respective programs and implications for the future of CHIP.[10]

We conducted this performance audit from November 2014 through February 2015 in accordance with generally accepted government auditing standards. Those standards require that we plan and perform our work to obtain sufficient, appropriate evidence to provide a reasonable basis for our findings and conclusions based on our audit objectives. We believe that the evidence obtained provides a reasonable basis for our findings and conclusions based on our audit objectives.

BACKGROUND

Federal law provides states with flexibility in how they operate their CHIP programs and how states implement more recent coverage options under PPACA. For example, states may operate CHIP as a separate program, include CHIP-eligible children in their Medicaid programs, or use a combination of the two approaches.[11] States with separate CHIP programs may modify certain aspects of their programs, such as coverage and cost-sharing requirements.[12] However, federal laws and regulations require states' separate CHIP programs to include coverage for routine check-ups, immunizations, inpatient and outpatient hospital services, and dental services defined as "necessary to prevent disease and promote oral health, restore oral structures to health and function, and treat emergency conditions."[13] In addition, CHIP premiums and cost-sharing may not exceed maximum amounts as defined by law.[14] Similarly, PPACA provides states with flexibility in how they opt to implement certain coverage options included in the law. For example, PPACA allows states to expand eligibility for Medicaid to most non-elderly, nonpregnant adults who are not eligible for Medicare and whose income is at or below 133 percent of the FPL.[15] As of January 2015, 29 states have implemented this expansion.[16] PPACA required the establishment of health insurance exchanges by January 1, 2014, to allow consumers to compare individual health insurance options available in each state and enroll in coverage. In states electing not to operate their own exchange, PPACA required the federal government to establish and operate an exchange in the state, referred to as a federally facilitated exchange. States with federally facilitated exchanges may enter into a partnership with HHS to assist with the operation of certain exchange functions. As such, a state could establish the exchange (referred to as a state-based exchange), cede the responsibility entirely to HHS (referred to as a federally facilitated exchange), or enter into a partnership with HHS (referred to as a partnership exchange).[17] As of January 2015, 17 states established state-based exchanges, 27 states were using the federally facilitated exchange, and 7 states established partnership exchanges.[18] See appendix 1 for information on the variation in children's uninsured rates, CHIP characteristics, and coverage approaches under PPACA by state.

The Children's Health Insurance Program Reauthorization Act of 2009 (CHIPRA) included provisions aimed at improving the information available from states on the quality of health care furnished to children in both CHIP and Medicaid.[19] Specifically, CHIPRA required the Secretary of HHS to conduct an independent evaluation of CHIP and to submit the results to Congress.[20] The mandated evaluation, for which the final report was issued in August 2014, documents what is known about CHIP; explores the program's evolution since inception; and examines the role CHIP has played in covering low-income children. In addition, CHIPRA required HHS to identify quality measures, known as the Child Core Set measures, to serve as a tool for states to use to monitor and improve the quality of health care provided to children enrolled in CHIP and Medicaid. CHIPRA also required HHS to develop a standardized format for states to voluntarily report these measures. These measures assess the quality of care provided through CHIP and Medicaid, and include a range of health conditions, such as asthma, obesity, attention deficit hyperactivity disorder, and perinatal care.[21] (See table 1.)

In 2013, as required by CHIPRA, HHS began annually publishing recommended changes to the Child Core Set measures in an effort to improve upon the measures and align them with national quality measurement activities, which can result in changes to the number of measures.[22]

Table 1. Child Core Set Measures by Clinical Area, 2014

Clinical area	Child Core Set measures
Access to care	• Children and adolescents' access to primary care practitioners
Acute care and chronic conditions	•Follow-up care for children prescribed attention-deficit hyperactivity disorder medication •Medication management for people with asthma
Behavioral health	•Behavioral health risk assessment (for pregnant women) •Follow-up after hospitalization for mental illness[a]
Consumer experience	•Consumer assessment of healthcare providers and systems health plan survey
Oral health	•Dental treatment services
	•Preventive dental services
Perinatal care	•Percentage of live births weighing less than 2,500 grams •Frequency of ongoing prenatal care •Cesarean rate for nulliparous singleton vertex •Timeliness of prenatal care •Pediatric central line-associated bloodstream infections
Preventive care and screening	•Development screening in the first three years of •life Body mass index assessment for children and adolescents
	•Chlamydia screening in women •Childhood immunization status
	•Immunization status for adolescents
	•Well-child visits in the first 15 months of life
	•Well-child visits in the third, fourth, fifth, and sixth years of life
	•Adolescent well-care visits
	•Human papillomavirus vaccine for female adolescents •Ambulatory care: emergency department visits

Source: Department of Health and Human Services. | GAO-15-348.

[a] States may elect to cover low-income pregnant women whose incomes are too high to qualify for Medicaid through their CHIP programs.

With the use of state reported data on the Child Core Set, HHS conducts an annual assessment and publishes its findings in its annual quality report, as required under CHIPRA.

States report CHIP service utilization and other measures through systems developed by HHS; specifically, the CHIP Annual Reporting Template System (CARTS), a web-based data submission tool, and through the Form CMS-416, an annual report submitted by states on the Medicaid Early and Periodic Screening, Diagnostic, and Treatment (EPSDT) benefit provided for enrolled children.[23] States that use managed care plans to deliver CHIP benefits are also required to report outcomes and performance measures from External Quality Review Organizations and performance improvement projects.[24]

CHIPRA also provided funding for the Quality Demonstration Grant Program to identify strategies for enhancing the quality of health care for children enrolled in Medicaid and CHIP.[25] HHS's AHRQ is evaluating the implementation of 52 projects in five general categories: (1) using quality measures to improve child health care; (2) applying health information technology for quality improvement; (3) implementing provider-based delivery models; (4) investigating the use of a model format for pediatric electronic health records, and (5) assessing the utility of other innovative approaches to enhance quality.

Assessments of National Data Largely Show Positive Effect of CHIP on Coverage and Access, and Identify Areas for Improvement

Available assessments of national data we reviewed identify positive effects of CHIP, including a reduction in the rate of uninsured children and children's improved access to care, and these findings are often consistent with our prior work. HHS also has ongoing efforts to enhance state reporting of the Child Core Set measures and publishes data from these quality measures to identify areas for improving the care provided in CHIP.

Mandated Evaluation Highlights Reduction in the Rate of Uninsured Children and Improved Access to Health Care

HHS's mandated evaluation identified several positive effects of CHIP across states, particularly with regard to children who are uninsured.[26] For example, based on an analysis of data from the Current Population Survey Annual Social and Economic Supplement (CPS-ASEC), the evaluation reported that Medicaid and CHIP contributed to the decline in the national rate of uninsured children between 1997 and 2012, with coverage rates improving for all ethnic and income groups.[27] Most notably, coverage rates for Hispanic children increased dramatically, rising from 42 percent to 65 percent during this time. Changes to state CHIP programs also contributed to the decline in the national uninsured rates among children. For example, many states expanded CHIP coverage by raising upper income eligibility limits and covering newly eligible groups, such as immigrant children who have resided legally in the United States for less than 5 years, which was newly permitted under federal law.[28] In addition, state outreach and enrollment activities also reduced the number of children eligible for—but not enrolled in—Medicaid or CHIP by about 1.2 million from 2008 to 2012.[29]

In addition, based on a survey of the parents of CHIP enrollees and disenrollees in a sample of states, the mandated evaluation also identified positive effects of CHIP with regard to access to services. For example, 96 percent of CHIP parents surveyed reported feeling confident that their child would be able to get needed health care, and 86 percent reported that their child had seen a doctor or health care professional in the last year.[30] The mandated evaluation further contrasted the experiences of CHIP enrollees who had been enrolled in CHIP for at least 12 months (referred to as CHIP enrollees) with the pre-CHIP experiences of two comparison groups: recent CHIP enrollees who were uninsured for at least 5 of the 12 months prior to enrollment (referred to as the uninsured), and recent CHIP enrollees who had 12 months of private coverage prior to enrollment (referred to as the privately insured). When compared to the uninsured children, the mandated evaluation found that CHIP enrollees reported having substantially better access to primary care, including preventive care, and higher utilization of covered services. For example,

- an estimated 88 percent of CHIP enrollees had a regular source of care compared with an estimated 78 percent of uninsured children;
- CHIP enrollees were an estimated 38 percentage points more likely to have a usual source of dental care, and were an estimated 39

percentage points more likely to have had a dental check-up in the past year;

- CHIP enrollees were an estimated 25 percentage points more likely to have an annual well-child checkup visit, and were more likely to receive a range of health services, including mental health visits, specialty care, and prescription drugs;
- CHIP enrollees were more likely to receive most preventive care measures, including flu vaccinations, vision screenings, and height and weight measurements; and
- parents of CHIP enrollees were less likely to report having trouble paying their child's medical bills, and were substantially more confident in their ability to get needed health care for their child.[31]

Based on our assessment of HHS's Medical Expenditure Panel Survey from 2007 through 2010, we also found that children enrolled in CHIP have better access to care and service use than children who are uninsured. In particular, when compared with uninsured children, we found that CHIP enrollees fared better, and the differences we identified were statistically significant in most cases.[32] For example, a higher proportion of CHIP respondents reported

- having a usual source of care; ease in getting a person the care, tests, or treatment that the parent or a doctor believed necessary; and ease in seeing a specialist; and
- using certain health care services, including office-based provider visits, outpatient department provider visits, and dental care visits.

When the mandated evaluation compared CHIP enrollees with the privately-insured group, it also found that CHIP enrollees experienced comparable access and service use for many, but not all, measures, and that parents of children enrolled in CHIP experienced less financial burden in paying their children's medical bills.

- CHIP enrollees used a similar level of preventive care and other health care services; however, CHIP enrollees had higher usage of prescription medication and lower levels of emergency department visits and hospital stays.

- CHIP enrollees had similar rates of health and development screenings, but were 9 percentage points less likely to receive a flu vaccination.
- CHIP enrollees had higher rates of dental access and utilization of certain services. For example, 92 percent of CHIP enrollees reported having access to dental coverage in 2012, compared with 77 percent of privately insured children. In terms of utilization, 84 percent of CHIP enrollees reported having a dental checkup or cleaning in the previous 12 months compared with 79 percent of privately insured children.
- Parents of CHIP enrollees reported substantially less trouble paying their children's medical bills and had much lower out-of-pocket spending levels.

For our assessment of the Medical Expenditure Panel Survey, we also compared CHIP enrollees' access and service use with children who were privately-insured, and our findings were consistent with some of the findings in the mandated evaluation.[33]

- When asked about access to care, we found that respondents with children enrolled in CHIP reported experiences that were generally comparable with privately insured children for 5 of the 6 measures reviewed, including having a usual source of care; ability to make needed appointments; and ease in seeing a specialist.[34]
- CHIP families faced a lower financial burden than families with private insurance because of the federal requirement that states' CHIP programs may not impose premiums and cost-sharing that, in the aggregate, exceed 5 percent of a family's total income for the length of the child's eligibility period.

However, with regard to the utilization of certain services, our prior work is less consistent with the findings of HHS's mandated evaluation.[35] For example, when asked about their use of certain medical and dental services, we found that access to care for CHIP enrollees was lower than that of the privately-insured for several services, and these differences were often statistically significant. Specifically, we previously reported that

- a lower proportion of CHIP enrollees reported visiting dentists (42.4 percent compared with 50.9 percent) and orthodontists (4.9 percent

compared with 11.2 percent) within the past 12 months than did those who were privately insured; and
- a higher proportion of CHIP enrollees reported having an emergency room visit (14.1 percent compared with 10.4 percent).

Differences between our findings and those included in the national evaluation may be related to the timeframes of the data and the measures used. For example, some of the data used in our analyses predate the CHIPRA requirement that CHIP programs offer comprehensive dental benefits coverage beginning in 2009. The timeframes for both bodies of work also predate the implementation of the PPACA requirement that most individual and small group market health plans provide pediatric dental coverage.

Finally, while the mandated evaluation noted that, overall, CHIP programs were meeting the health care needs of most enrollees, it identified areas for program improvement. Specifically, many CHIP enrollees did not receive recommended preventive care or reported an unmet health care need. For example, slightly less than half of CHIP enrollees received a flu vaccination, and only about one-third received a developmental screening for children under age 6. In addition, one in four CHIP enrollees had an unmet health care need, with the highest unmet need being for dental care.

HHS Has Ongoing Efforts to Enhance State Reporting of Quality Measures and Identify Areas for Improvement to Care Provided in CHIP

HHS publishes data that states report on the Child Core Set measures in its annual quality report. While reporting on the Child Core Set measures is voluntary for states, the number of states reporting these quality measures and the median number of measures each state reports has increased steadily since reporting of the measures began in 2010. For example, beginning in fiscal year 2012, all 51 states have reported at least two or more measures, a notable increase from the 43 states that reported at least one measure for fiscal year 2010.[36] Similarly, the median number of Child Core Set measures that states report has increased from about 7 measures in fiscal year 2010 to 16 measures in fiscal year 2013. HHS attributed the rise in state reporting to increased familiarity with the Child Core Set measures and the department's efforts to streamline state reporting and provide technical assistance and guidance to states. For example, CMS established a Quality Measures Technical

Assistance and Analytic Support Program in May 2011, which works with states to support their efforts in collecting, reporting, and using quality measures for their CHIP and Medicaid programs.

However, states varied considerably in the number of measures they reported in fiscal year 2013, ranging from 2 measures in Nebraska and Wisconsin to 25 measures in North Carolina and South Carolina. (See fig. 1.)

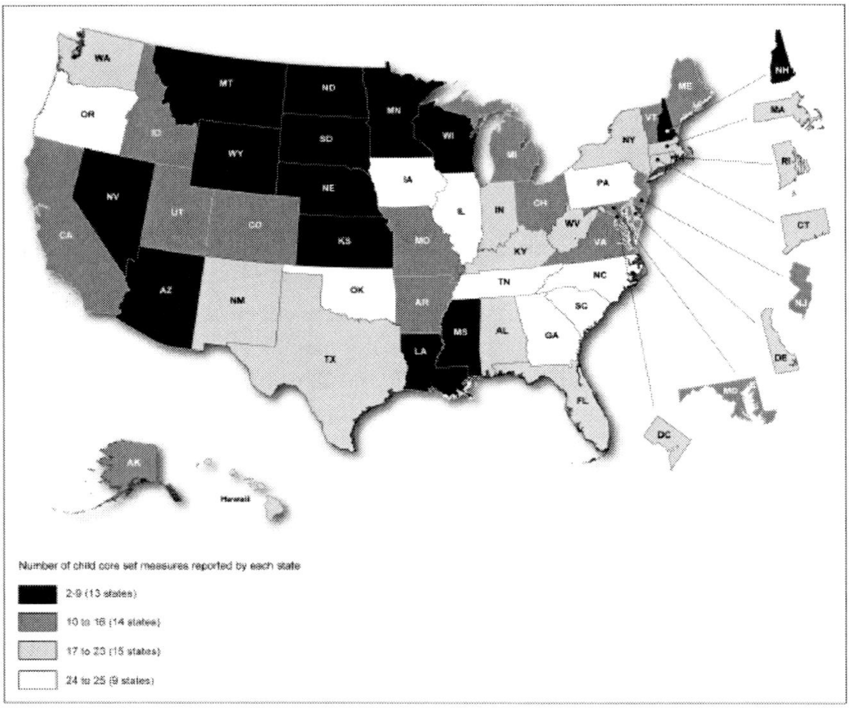

Source: Department of Health and Human Services (Data); Map Resources (map). | GAO-15-348.

Figure 1. Number of Child Core Set Measures Reported by States in Fiscal Year 2013.

Several factors can affect a state's ability to report the Child Core Set measures. Officials from the states we reviewed provided the following examples of challenges they face reporting the Child Core Set measures.

- Mississippi and Pennsylvania officials cited difficulty reporting certain measures, such as the extent of follow-up care for children prescribed medication for attention-deficit/hyperactivity disorder, due, in part, to their not having access to the data required to report the measure.[37]

- Arizona, New Hampshire, Nevada, and Wisconsin officials cited the difficulty and cost of reporting certain measures, in particular those measures that require medical record reviews as opposed to the reporting of measures that use only encounter data.[38] For example, HHS suggests that medical record reviews be used to calculate a perinatal measure related to the performance of caesarean sections and none of these states reported this measure in fiscal year 2013.[39]
- Rhode Island officials noted that it can be difficult to collect data for measures that are not nationally endorsed—and as a result, they may not report them. For example, in fiscal year 2013, Rhode Island did not report the Child Core Set measure of a developmental screening in the first 3 years of a child's life, which had not been endorsed by the National Committee for Quality Assurance, but developed by a university in Oregon.
- Noting that the state does not have a department dedicated to measuring quality, Alaska cited a lack of internal expertise needed to collect and report reliable data for the measures. As such, an official cited the need to leverage resources and work with other agencies within the state that have the expertise to analyze measures and set targets for quality improvement.

In light of difficulties cited by states in reporting on the Child Core Set measures, HHS reported ongoing efforts to assist states with reporting the measures. For example, to streamline state reporting, HHS began calculating three Child Core Set measures on behalf of states in fiscal year 2012. Specifically, HHS began calculating the preventive dental and dental treatment measures from the Form CMS-416. At this time, HHS also began using data available from the Centers for Disease Control and Prevention to calculate the neonatal central-line associated blood stream infection measure. In addition, HHS assists states by allowing states to report Child Core Set measures for the Medicaid population, CHIP population, or combined Medicaid and CHIP populations.

Additionally, HHS reported efforts to assist states in improving their reporting of the Child Core Set measures through the Quality Demonstration Grant Program.[40] Through this program, HHS awarded 10 grants providing funding to 18 states to implement various projects to improve the information available on the quality of care provided to children enrolled in CHIP, including undertaking efforts to improve their reporting of the Child Core Set measures. For example, in one such project, Pennsylvania is testing the use of financial rewards to encourage certain health systems—which include hospitals, primary care practice sites, and other facilities—to use the Child Core Set measures to drive quality improvement projects.[41] Pennsylvania also reported that it is recruiting health systems to determine the extent to which electronic health records can provide data for the Child Core Set measures for children.[42]

From the measures submitted by states, HHS reports states' performance to assess the quality of care for children enrolled in CHIP and Medicaid, and the results of this assessment are mixed.[43] HHS calculates mean rates for most of the Child Core Set measures—which it calls performance rates—including primary and preventive care, perinatal health, management of acute and chronic conditions, and dental services, among the states reporting those measures.[44] Based on this assessment, HHS determined that states had high performance rates for some measures, such as young children's access to primary care. For example, a mean of 96 percent of children aged 12 to 24 months enrolled in CHIP or Medicaid had at least one primary care physician visit during fiscal year 2013.[45] In contrast, states had lower performance rates for other measures. For example, a mean of 46 percent of children received at least one preventive dental service, and a mean of 25 percent of children received at least one dental treatment in fiscal year 2013.[46] (See table 2.) As such, HHS specified that children's access to oral health care continues to be a primary focus of improvement efforts in CHIP and Medicaid.

Table 2. Mean Performance Rates and Number of States Reporting Certain Child Core Set Measures, Fiscal Year 2013

Child Core Set measure	Mean performance rate	Number of states reporting measure
Children's (aged 12 to 24 months) access to primary care practitioners	96[a]	45
Timeliness of prenatal care	77	33
Appropriate testing for children with pharyngitis[b]	68	36
Well-child visits in the 3rd, 4th, 5th, and 6th years of life	66	47
Childhood immunization status	64	30
Immunization status for adolescents	63	30
Well-child visits in the first 15 months of life	60	44

Child Core Set measure	Mean performance rate	Number of states reporting measure
Frequency of ongoing prenatal care	56	27
Chlamydia screening in women	49	37
Follow-up care for children prescribed attention-deficit/hyperactivity disorder medication	46[c]	31
Follow-up after hospitalization for mental illness	47[d]	27
Preventive dental services[e]	46	49
Adolescent well-care visits	45	43
Body mass index assessment for children and adolescents	34	25
Dental treatment services[e]	25	49

Source: Department of Health and Human Services (HHS). | GAO-15-348

Note: This table reports the mean performance rates for the most frequently reported Child Core Set measures in fiscal year 2013. These rates represent service utilization for State Children's Health Insurance Program (CHIP) and Medicaid enrollees. Rates were rounded up to the nearest whole number.

[a] HHS also reported mean performance rates for children aged 25 months to 6 years, aged 7 to 11 years, and aged 12 to 19 years. About 88 percent of children in each of these age groups had at least one primary care physician visit during fiscal year 2013.

[b] HHS retired this measure from the Child Core Set in 2014.

[c] The table reports the mean performance rate for follow up visits for children prescribed medication for attention deficit hyperactivity disorder during the first 30 days of an initial visit in fiscal year 2013. The mean performance rate for follow up visits for children prescribed such medication within the first 90 days of an initial visit is 54 percent.

[d] The table reports the mean performance rate for follow up visits for children with mental illness within 7 days. The mean performance rate for follow up visits within 30 days is 65 percent.

[e] HHS began reporting Child Core Set measures on behalf of states from data states submit on the Form CMS-416 in fiscal year 2012. Data on these measures include children enrolled in Medicaid and CHIP Medicaid expansion programs, but does not include children enrolled in separate CHIP programs.

In addition to HHS's review of states' reporting on the Child Core Set measures, the department's annual quality report includes the results of its review of external quality review reports and performance improvement projects from states that contract with managed care plans to deliver services for CHIP and Medicaid enrollees.[47] States are required to annually review their managed care plans to evaluate the quality, timeliness, and access to services that the plans provide to enrollees, and HHS must include this information in its annual quality report. For the most recent annual quality report, 40 of the 42 states that contract with managed care plans to deliver services to CHIP and Medicaid enrollees submitted external quality review reports.[48] Based on its review of these reports, HHS found that the most frequently reported performance measures from states' external quality reports—which included well-child care, primary care access, childhood immunization rates, and prenatal/postpartum care—mirrored states' most frequently reported Child Core Set measures in fiscal year 2013. In terms of HHS's review of states' performance improvement projects, 38 of the 40 states that submitted external quality review reports included at least one project targeted to improve the quality of care for children and pregnant women enrolled in managed care; for example, by implementing projects related to behavioral health and improving childhood immunization rates for children, and prenatal and postpartum care for pregnant women.

Cost, Coverage, and Access to Care Are Key Considerations in Determining the Reauthorization of CHIP Funding

Our prior work has identified important considerations related to cost, coverage, and access when determining the ongoing need for CHIP, many of which were echoed by officials from the 10 states we reviewed. With regard to cost, our prior work comparing CHIP plans to states' benchmark plans, which were the models for health plans available under health insurance exchanges established under PPACA, found that costs—defined as deductibles, copayments, coinsurance, and premiums—were almost always less for CHIP plans.[49]

- CHIP plans we reviewed typically did not require the payment of deductibles, while all five states' benchmark plans did.[50]
- The cost difference in copayments between CHIP plans and benchmark plans was considerable for physician visits, prescription drugs, and outpatient therapies. For example, an office visit to a specialist in Colorado would cost a CHIP enrollee $2 to $10 per visit, depending on their income, compared to $50 per visit for benchmark plan enrollees.

- Families could face higher dental costs in states where dental coverage through the exchange is optional and offered as a standalone dental plan (SADP) as opposed to CHIP plans where dental benefits are included.[51]

Officials from five selected states also expressed concerns about the higher costs of QHP coverage and the implications this would have for families.

- Based on a review of QHPs available on the state's exchange in 2014, Nevada officials estimated that the average annual premium for a child in a family with an income of 168 percent of the FPL was more than two and a half times higher than the $200 premium for coverage in a CHIP plan. This price difference does not account for differences in co-pays, which the state does not charge under CHIP.[52] The extent to which QHPs in the state apply co-pays to covered services could increase this price differential further. As such, Nevada officials were concerned that absent CHIP, families would not purchase QHP plans due to their higher cost.[53]
- Due to the additional premiums and cost-sharing associated with SADPs, New Hampshire officials expressed concern that families will forego dental care if they must purchase a SADP.[54] The officials noted that cost-sharing particularly affects families with incomes from 185 to 250 percent of the FPL, which is 75 percent of the state's CHIP population.

We also previously reported that coverage is a relevant consideration, and that separate CHIP and benchmark plans were generally similar in terms of their coverage of selected services and the services on which they imposed limits, with some variation. 55 For example, the plans we reviewed were similar in that they typically did not impose any limits on ambulatory patient services, emergency care, preventive care, or prescription drugs; but commonly imposed limits on outpatient therapies, and pediatric dental, vision, and hearing services. Officials from several selected states pointed out that CHIP coverage was more comprehensive than QHPs for certain services, particularly for services needed by children with special health care needs.

- Alaska and Pennsylvania officials noted that coverage of services—including orthodontics, vision, audiology, outpatient therapies, language disorders, and durable medical equipment—was more comprehensive in CHIP when compared with QHPs in their states.

- Rhode Island officials highlighted the state's coverage of comprehensive pediatric dental services and any medically necessary services deemed warranted as a result of the EPSDT benefit to which all CHIP-eligible children in the state are entitled. According to the state officials, these same services are either unavailable or unaffordable through QHPs in the state.
- Arizona officials specified that coverage of certain enabling services, such as non-emergency medical transportation, family support services, and behavioral health services are included in the state's CHIP plan, but may not be offered in QHPs.[56]

With regard to access, our work found that CHIP enrollees generally reported positive responses in their ability to obtain care that was generally comparable to those with private insurance, with some exceptions, including lower utilization of dental and orthodontia services. Some of the states we reviewed also raised concerns related to access to care if CHIP funding is not reauthorized. For example, Nevada officials raised concerns about the ability of certain populations—specifically, children of undocumented parents—to access care if CHIP is no longer available. Nevada officials stated that these children could lose CHIP coverage since a significant portion of them have parents who may not file federal income tax returns that would expose them to tax penalties for failing to enroll their children in alternative health coverage. In addition, an Alaska official noted the need for further work on the comparability of benefits between QHPs and CHIP to ensure that the former could be an adequate substitute, and that children moving to QHPs would not experience decreased access to health care. The official noted that comparability across benefit packages is particularly important for children in households whose income changes would result in movement between CHIP and QHPs.

AGENCY COMMENTS

We provided a draft of this report to HHS for comment. The department provided technical comments, which we incorporated as appropriate.

Carolyn L. Yocom, Director, Health Care

APPENDIX I: UNINSURED RATES, STATE APRAHESCHILDREN'S HEALTH INSURANCE PROGRAM (CHIP) CHARACTERISTICS, AND COVERAGE APPROACHES

State	Percentage ofuninsured children in 2013	Design of state program under CHIP[a]	CHIP enroll-ment in 2013	CHIP upper incomeeligibi-lity standard (percent of theFPL), as of 2014[b]	Whether the state expandedMedicaid to newlyeligible adultsunder the Patient Protection and Affordable Care Act (PPACA)	State health insurance marketplace design, 2015
Alabama	4.3	Combination	113,490	312	No	Federally facilitated
Alaska	11.6	CHIP Medicaid expansion	16,566	203	No	Federally facilitated
Arizona	11.9	Combination	80,238	200	Yes	Federally facilitated
Arkansas	5.5	Combination	109,301	211	Yes	Partnership
California	7.4	Combination	1,603,283	261	Yes	State-based
Colorado	8.2	Combination	90,397	260	Yes	State-based
Connecti-cut	4.3	Separate	18,999	318	Yes	State-based
Delaware	4.5	Combination	13,180	212	Yes	Partnership
District of Columbia	2.4 CHIP	Medicaid expansion	9,057	319	Yes	State-based
Florida	11.1	Combination	473,415	210	No	Federally facilitated
Georgia	9.6	Combination	269,906	247	No	Federally facilitated
Hawaii	3.0	CHIP Medicaid xpansion[c]	30,979	308	Yes	State-based
Idaho	8.9	Combination	45,399	185	No	State-based
Illinois	4.2	Combination	337,097	313	Yes	Partnership
Indiana	8.2	Combination	152,415	250	Yes	Federally facilitated
Iowa	4.1	Combination	83,670	302	Yes	Partnership
Kansas	6.1	Combination	76,164	242	No	Federally facilitated
Kentucky	5.9	Combination	84,069	213	Yes	State-based
Louisiana	5.7	Combination	149,968	250	No	Federally facilitated
Maine	5.9	Combination	29,712	208	No	Federally facilitated

Appendix I. (Continued)

State	Percentage ofuninsured children in 2013	Design of state program under CHIPa	CHIP enroll-ment in 2013	CHIP upper incomeeligibi-lity standard (percent of theFPL), as of 2014[b]	Whether the state expandedMedicaid to newlyeligible adultsunder the Patient Protection and Affordable Care Act (PPACA)	State health insurance marketplace design, 2015
Maryland	4.4	CHIP Medicaid expansion	135,454	317	Yes	State-based
Massa-chusetts	1.5	Combination	148,719	300	Yes	State-based
Michigan	4.0	Combination	89,670	212	Yes	Partnership
Minnesota	5.6	Combination	3,835	283c	Yes	State-based
Mississi-ppi	7.6	Combination	93,120	209	No	Federally facilitated
Missouri	7.0	Combination	92,918	300	No	Federally facilitated
Montana	10.1	Combination	44,661	261	No	Federally facilitated
Nebraska	5.5	Combination	55,783	213	No	Federally facilitated
Nevada	14.9	Combination	28,626	200	Yes	State based[d]
New Hamp-shire	3.8	CHIP Medicaid expansion	19,450	318	Yes	Partnership
New Jersey	5.6	Combination	206,761	350	Yes	Federally facilitated
New Mexico	8.5	CHIP Medicaid expansion	9,368	300c	Yes	State based[d]
New York	4.0	Combination	490,114	400	Yes	State-based
North Carolina	6.3	Combination	260,964	211	No	Federally facilitated
North Dakota	7.9	Combination	11,281	170	Yes	Federally facilitated
Ohio	5.3	CHIP Medicaid expansion	286,817	206	Yes	Federally facilitated
Oklahoma	10.0	Combination	147,911	205	No	Federally facilitated
Oregon	5.8	Combination	128,061	300	Yes	State based[d]
Pennsyl-vania	5.4	Combination	267,073	314	Yes	Federally facilitated
Rhode Island	5.4	Combination	26,577	261	Yes	State-based

State	Percentage ofuninsured children in 2013	Design of state program under CHIPa	CHIP enroll-ment in 2013	CHIP upper incomeeligibi-lity standard (percent of theFPL), as of 2014[b]	Whether the state expandedMedicaid to newlyeligible adultsunder the Patient Protection and Affordable Care Act (PPACA)	State health insurance marketplace design, 2015
South Carolina	6.7	CHIP Medicaid expansion	76,191	208	No	Federally facilitated
South Dakota	6.3	Combination	17,632	204	No	Federally facilitated
Tennessee	5.7	Combination	106,473	250	No	Federally facilitated
Texas	12.6	Combination	1,034,613	201	No	Federally facilitated
Utah	9.5	Combination	63,001	200	No	Federally facilitated
Vermont	3.1 CHIP	Medicaid expansion	7,393	312	Yes	State-based
Virginia	5.4	Combination	196,911	200	No	Federally facilitated
Washing-ton	5.9	Separate	44,073	312	Yes	State-based
West Virginia	5.3	Combination	37,065	300	Yes	Partnership
Wisconsin	4.7	Combination	167,292	301	No	Federally facilitated
Wyoming	5.7	Combination	8,815	200	No	Federally facilitated

Source: GAO based on information from the Centers for Medicare & Medicaid Services (CMS), as of February 2015; State Medicaid and State Children's Health Insurance Program (CHIP) Income eligibility Standards as of October 1, 2014; The Henry J. Kaiser Family Foundation, State Health Insurance Marketplace Types, 2015; U.S. Census Bureau, 2013 American Community Survey. | GAO-15-348

[a] As of February 2015, 42 states operated separate CHIP programs (2 states had a separate CHIP program only, and 40 states covered CHIP children through both a separate program and an expansion of their Medicaid program). The other 9 states covered CHIP children through an expansion of their Medicaid program, which we refer to as a "CHIP Medicaid expansion."

[b] PPACA specifies that an income disregard equal to 5 percentage points of the federal poverty level (FPL) be deducted from an individual's income when determining Medicaid and CHIP eligibility. The FPL eligibility standards in this table do not reflect this income disregard.

[c] Minnesota and New Mexico have CHIP income eligibility levels that vary by age group; therefore, we reported the highest income eligibility level reported for these states—which are ages 0 to 1 year in Minnesota and ages 0 to 5 years in New Mexico.

[d] These state-based marketplaces use the federally facilitated marketplace's information technology platform for applicants to apply and enroll in their respective states.

End Notes

[1] See GAO, Health Insurance for Children: Private Insurance Coverage Continues to Deteriorate, GAO/HEHS-96-129 (Washington, D.C.: June 17, 1996).

[2] The uninsured rate for children varies considerably among states. See Cohen, R.A, Martinez, M.E., Health Insurance Coverage: Early Release of Estimates from the National Health Interview Survey, January-March 2014.

[3] Most states' CHIP eligibility levels are between 200 and 300 percent of the federal poverty level (FPL), with the highest eligibility level being 400 percent of the FPL.

[4] Pub. L. No. 111-148, § 10203, 124 Stat. 119, 927 (2010). In this report, references to PPACA include any amendments made by the Health Care and Education Reconciliation Act of 2010, Pub. L. No. 111-152, 124 Stat. 1029 (2010), unless otherwise indicated.

[5] Although federal appropriations for the program will end on September 30, 2015, any unexpended amounts allotted to the states in fiscal year 2015 will be available for expenditure through September 30, 2016.

[6] PPACA required the establishment of health insurance exchanges by January 1, 2014—marketplaces where eligible individuals can compare and select among QHPs offered by participating private issuers of health coverage. The Secretary is required to report by April 2015 on comparability of benefits and cost sharing between CHIP and QHPs. As of January 2015, CMS had not issued guidance on how comparability between QHPs and CHIP will be defined. CHIP regulations also generally require that, for children found ineligible for CHIP, either at the time of initial application or during a follow-up eligibility determination, the state must screen the child for Medicaid eligibility and, if ineligible for Medicaid, the state must then screen for potential eligibility for other insurance affordability programs, including subsidized coverage in a QHP.

[7] To carry out this mandated evaluation, HHS used the services of a contractor, Mathematica Policy Research, and its subcontractor, the Urban Institute. See Mathematica Policy Research and Urban Institute, CHIPRA Mandated Evaluation of the Children's Health Insurance Program: Final Findings (Washington, D.C.: Aug. 1, 2014), located at http://aspe.hhs.gov/health/reports/2014/chipevaluation/rpt_chipevaluation.pdf. The findings included in this national evaluation were based on multiple sources of data, including a survey of CHIP program administrators; state eligibility and enrollment data; and a survey of CHIP enrollees and disenrollees in 10 states: Alabama, California, Florida, Louisiana, Michigan, New York, Ohio, Texas, Utah, and Virginia. An interim report on the evaluation was delivered to Congress in December 2011.

[8] For HHS's most recent report see The Department of Health and Human Services, 2014 Annual Report on the Quality of Care for Children in Medicaid and CHIP (Washington, D.C.: Nov.

2014). The issue briefs that we reviewed are published by HHS's Agency for Healthcare Research and Quality (AHRQ) and are available at http://www.ahrq.gov/policymakers/chipra/demoeval/what-we-learned/index.html (accessed December 18, 2014).

[9] In selecting states, we also excluded those with fewer than 10,000 children and states that were included in the Mathematica review. Our findings related to information collected from these states cannot be generalized.

[10] In July 2014, the Senate Finance Committee and the House Energy and Commerce Committee sent a joint letter to state governors requesting information on their CHIP programs, as well as their thoughts on extending CHIP funding and any additional policy changes that could be made to the program. The committees released states' responses on December 3, 2014. These responses are available at http://energycommerce.house. gov/letter/responses-bipartisan-bicameral-lettersgovernors-regarding-chip (accessed January 21, 2015).

[11] As of February 2015, 42 states operated separate CHIP programs (2 states had a separate CHIP program only and 40 states covered CHIP children through both a separate program and an expansion of their Medicaid program). The other 9 states covered CHIP children through an expansion of their Medicaid program, which we refer to as a "CHIP Medicaid expansion." States' CHIP spending has been reimbursed by the federal government at a matching rate that is generally about 15 percent higher than the Medicaid rate and varies by states, ranging from 65 percent for the wealthiest state to about 82 percent for the poorest state in 2015.

[12] States that opt to include CHIP-eligible children in their Medicaid programs must extend Medicaid covered services to them.

[13] 42 U.S.C. § 1397cc(c).

[14] For example, states may not impose premiums and cost-sharing, in the aggregate, that exceed 5 percent of a family's total income for the length of the child's eligibility period in CHIP. This annual cumulative cost-sharing maximum applies to all services with cost-sharing requirements, irrespective of the number of children in the family that are enrolled in CHIP.

[15] PPACA, § 2001(a)(1),124 Stat. 119, 271 (2010). PPACA also imposes a 5 percent income disregard when calculating modified adjusted gross income, which, in effect, raises this income limit to 138 percent of the FPL.

[16] For purposes of this report, we consider the District of Columbia as a state. The Henry J. Kaiser Family Foundation, "Medicaid Moving Forward," (Menlo Park, CA: January 2015).

[17] A partnership exchange is a variation of a federally facilitated exchange. HHS will establish and operate this type of exchange with states assisting HHS to carry out certain functions of that exchange.

[18] The Henry J. Kaiser Family Foundation, State Health Insurance Marketplace Types, 2015, accessed January 7, 2015, http://Kff.org/health-reform/state-indicator/state-healthinsurance-marketplace-types/#table.

[19] Pub. L. No. 111-3, 123 Stat. 8 (2009) (hereafter, "CHIPRA").

[20] CHIPRA, § 603, 123 Stat. at 99. The CHIPRA mandated evaluation was patterned after an earlier evaluation mandated in the Balanced Budget Refinement Act (BBRA) of 1999.

[21] CHIPRA also requires state CHIP programs to report annually on quality of care and consumer satisfaction measures included in the Consumer Assessment of Healthcare Providers and Systems (CAHPS) surveys. States can choose among the available types of CAHPS surveys to address this requirement, but HHS recommends that they use the version listed in the Child Core Set measures. The survey, developed by HHS's AHRQ, asks consumers and patients to report on and evaluate their experiences with health care.

[22] For example, HHS recommended that three measures be retired from the 2014 Child Core Set: appropriate testing for children with pharyngitis, asthma patients with one or more asthma-

related emergency room visits, and annual pediatric hemoglobin A1c testing. In addition, an HHS-funded National Qualify Forum workgroup convenes a public-private partnership to provide input to HHS on the selection of performance measures for public reporting and performance-based payment programs. The public-private partnership makes recommendations to HHS for strengthening and revising measures in the Child Core Set.

[23] State Medicaid programs are required to cover EPSDT benefits for children under age 21. EPSDT benefits include comprehensive screenings, preventive health care services, and other services necessary to correct illnesses or conditions identified by the screenings. The Form CMS-416 is an annual report submitted by states on EPSDT benefits provided for children who are enrolled in Medicaid.

[24] States are required to perform an annual external quality review for each contracted managed care plan and prepaid inpatient health plan, which includes information and analysis of quality outcomes and performance measures for the populations served by the plans.

[25] In February 2010, CMS awarded 10 grants—which funded 18 states to implement projects that include using quality measures to improve child health. CMS also provided funding to AHRQ to lead a national evaluation of these demonstrations, to be completed by September 30, 2015.

[26] See Mathematica Policy Research and Urban Institute, CHIPRA Mandated Evaluation of the Children's Health Insurance Program: Final Findings (Washington, D.C.: Aug. 1, 2014).

[27] According to the mandated evaluation, the percentage of all children who were uninsured fell from 15 percent in 1997 to 9 percent in 2012. Further, among low-income children, the percentage of uninsured fell from 25 percent in 1997 to 13 percent in 2012. For purposes of this evaluation, low-income children were defined as children between the ages of 0 and 18, with income below 200 percent of the FPL. The mandated evaluation relied on the CPS-ASEC, which provided time series of data on health insurance coverage over the 15-year period—1997 through 2012—since CHIP's enactment.

[28] For example, CHIPRA allowed states to expand CHIP eligibility to include legally residing immigrant children and pregnant women, regardless of how long they have been legally residing in the United States. As of August 2014, 24 states expanded CHIP eligibility to include one or both of these groups. In addition, PPACA allowed states to expand CHIP eligibility to include children of low-income state employees, which had been previously prohibited. As of August 2014, 16 states had extended CHIP eligibility to children of state employees.

[29] While GAO has not estimated the effect of CHIP on the uninsured rate of children, the mandated evaluation notes that previous research has also documented substantial declines in the uninsured rate among low-income children following CHIP's implementation.

[30] To determine whether factors other than insurance coverage may affect differences in responses about obtaining care or utilization of health care services, the mandated evaluation controlled for age, sex, race/ethnicity and language groups, more than three children in the household, highest education of any parent, parents' employment status, parent citizenship, and local area or county.

[31] We previously reported that lower-income households paid a larger percentage of their income on premiums, with households with incomes below 227 percent of the FPL paying 7.3 percent of their income on premiums. See GAO-09-252.

[32] See GAO-14-40. In conducting our logistic regressions, we controlled for the following factors: age, race, income, total number of parents in the household, parent education, family size, health status, mental health status, children with special needs, total number of

workers in the household, metropolitan statistical area, sex, whether the respondent was born in the United States, and English versus non-English speakers.

33 To describe access to care for children in CHIP compared with those with Medicaid, private insurance, or without insurance, we analyzed nationwide data from HHS's Medical Expenditure Panel Survey from 2007 through 2010.

34 Respondents' reported ease in getting needed care was the only measure for which we identified a statistically significant difference.

35 See GAO-14-40.

36 There were 24 Child Core Set measures in both fiscal years 2010 and 2012.

37 The Mississippi official told us that the state was in the process of hiring a contractor to collect data that were previously unavailable to the state.

38 There are different types of quality measures—such as structural, process, outcome, and patient experience—and measures of each type vary greatly in their breadth. Additionally, the data used to apply these different types of measures can come from a number of sources. Clinical data extracted from medical records can provide important clinical details needed to more fully adjust provider performance assessments for differences in the severity of illness of the patients that they treat—a process known as risk adjustment—but such data are typically costly and time-consuming to collect. By contrast, claims data—also known as billing or administrative data—are already collected to process provider payments, and therefore are more readily available for a large number of patients. However, because claims data are collected for payment purposes, they contain only a limited set of information relevant for quality measures or for making risk adjustments. Encounter data are records of services delivered to beneficiaries enrolled in managed care plans that receive a per-member-per-month payment. See GAO, Health Care Transparency: Actions Needed to Improve Cost and Quality, GAO-15-11 (Washington, D.C.: Oct. 20, 2014).

39 Wisconsin also noted that it only reported on two Child Core Set measures in fiscal year 2013 due to HHS's deadline to report the information.

40 While AHRQ anticipates releasing a final evaluation of the state activities in the fall of 2015, it has issued 10 issue briefs that provide preliminary findings on the activities participating states are pursing to improve the quality and delivery systems for children's health care. These briefs can be found at http://www.ahrq.gov/policymakers/chipra/demoeval/what-we-learned/index.html (accessed December 18, 2014).

41 According to AHRQ, participating health systems are financially rewarded for reporting any Child Core Set measures from electronic health records and for improved reporting on a subset of such measures. Health systems generally use their financial rewards to fund quality improvement projects related to the Child Core Set measures.

42 Five health systems are participating in Pennsylvania's model format of pediatric health records project, including three children's hospitals and affiliated ambulatory practice sites, one federally qualified health center, and one small hospital.

43 HHS contracted with Mathematica to provide technical assistance to the states in submitting their data for the Child Core Set measures.

44 With analytic and technical assistance support available from Mathematica, states submit numerator and denominator information on the Child Core Set measures, and attest to the accuracy of the quality measure being reported to HHS.

45 HHS also reported mean performance rates for children ages 25 months to 6 years, aged 7 to 11 years, and aged 12 to 19 years. About 88 percent of children in each of these age groups had at least one primary care physician visit during fiscal year 2013.

[46] The dental measures in the Child Core Set are obtained from the Form CMS-416, which reports on the receipt of EPSDT benefits for children in Medicaid. Therefore, the measures include children aged 1 to 20 enrolled in Medicaid and CHIP Medicaid expansion programs, but may not include children enrolled in separate CHIP programs. Additionally, these are separate performance rates for dental preventive and dental treatment services, whereas the mandated evaluation reported the percentage of children that had any type of dental visit. HHS officials also specified that the preventive dental services measure includes only those preventive services performed by or under the supervision of a dentist—and do not include oral health services, such as fluoride varnish, performed by non-dental professionals. As such, HHS officials noted that in most states these data undercount the extent to which enrollees are receiving preventive dental and oral health services.

[47] About 66 percent of publicly insured children obtained care through managed care plans in fiscal year 2013.

[48] According to the annual quality report, two states did not submit their external quality review reports by a specified timeframe for inclusion in HHS's analysis.

[49] To prepare for the offering of QHPs in 2014, HHS asked states to select benchmark health plans—plans intended as models for the benefits that will be offered through QHPs—by December 26, 2012.

[50] See GAO-14-40. The five states evaluated in our prior work were Colorado, Illinois, Kansas, New York, and Utah. These findings were subsequently discussed in a hearing before the Subcommittee on Health, Committee on Energy and Commerce, House of Representatives on December 3, 2014. See GAO, Children's Health Insurance: Cost, Coverage, and Access Considerations for Extending Federal Funding. GAO-15-268T (Washington, D.C.: Dec. 3, 2014); We are currently examining how CHIP coverage and consumer costs compare to selected QHPs that were available on the exchanges in these five states in 2014.

[51] PPACA allows exchanges in each state the option of providing pediatric dental services using a SADP. In exchanges with at least one participating SADP, the QHPs have the option of excluding pediatric dental benefits from their covered services.

[52] Additionally, Nevada officials indicated that under CHIP, premiums—which are determined based on family size and income—are charged per family, not per child. Thus, CHIP costs do not increase by the number of children covered, as they would under a QHP. Up to three covered children may be taken into account in determining family premiums for QHPs.

[53] PPACA requires that most individuals, subject to certain exceptions, obtain health insurance coverage or pay a federal tax penalty, known as a shared responsibility payment. Among other exceptions, individuals for whom the cost of coverage is considered unaffordable are not subject to the penalty.

[54] SADPs have out-of-pocket maximum costs that are in addition to the QHP maximum costs, which may increase potential maximum costs for families who purchase them.

[55] See GAO-14-40. We reviewed the following services: ambulatory patient services (primary care physician and specialist office visits, and outpatient surgery); emergency care; inpatient physician and specialist office visits, and outpatient surgery); emergency care; inpatient hospital services (facility, professional, and ancillary); maternity care; mental health services (inpatient and outpatient); substance abuse services (inpatient and outpatient); prescription drugs; preventive care (well-child care, immunizations, and chronic disease management); outpatient therapies (physical, speech, and occupational for rehabilitation and habilitation); pediatric dental services (routine, emergency, and other); pediatric vision services (exams and corrective lenses); laboratory services (inpatient and outpatient);

pediatric hearing services (testing and hearing aids); durable medical equipment; hospice; and home and community-based health care.

[56] Enabling services, such as case management/care coordination, non-emergency transportation, and translation services, are services that are designed to increase the accessibility of primary and preventive health care services for eligible low-income individuals. Enabling services are generally used to reduce nonfinancial barriers and to facilitate access to care among lower income populations.

In: State Children's Health Insurance Program
Editor: Ted Warner
ISBN: 978-1-63483-673-9

Chapter 2

CHILDREN'S HEALTH INSURANCE: COVERAGE OF SERVICES AND COSTS TO CONSUMERS IN SELECTED CHIP AND PRIVATE HEALTH PLANS IN FIVE STATES*

United States Government Accountability Office

WHY GAO DID THIS STUDY

Federal funds appropriated to states for CHIP—the jointly financed health insurance program for certain low-income children—are expected to be exhausted soon after the end of fiscal year 2015 unless Congress acts to appropriate new funds. Beginning in October 2015, any state with insufficient CHIP funding must establish procedures to ensure that children who are not covered by CHIP are screened for Medicaid eligibility. If ineligible, children may be enrolled into a private qualified health plan—or QHP—that has been certified by the Secretary of Health and Human Services (HHS) as comparable to CHIP, if such a QHP is available.

GAO was asked to examine coverage and costs to consumers in selected CHIP plans and private QHPs in selected states. GAO reviewed (1) coverage and (2) costs to consumers for one CHIP plan, one QHP, and, where

---

* This is an edited, reformatted and augmented version of a United States Government Accountability Office publication, No. GAO-15-323, dated February 2015.

applicable, one SADP in each of five states— Colorado, Illinois, Kansas, New York, and Utah. State selection was based on variation in location, program size, and design; CHIP plan selection was based on high enrollment; and QHP selection was based on low plan premiums. GAO obtained CHIP and QHP premium data from state officials and federal and state websites. GAO also obtained documents from and spoke to federal officials, including from HHS's Assistant Secretary for Planning and Evaluation, state officials, including from CHIP and insurance departments, and issuers of QHPs.

HHS provided technical comments on a draft of this report, which GAO incorporated as appropriate.

WHAT GAO FOUND

In five selected states, GAO determined that coverage of services in the selected State Children's Health Insurance Program (CHIP) plans was generally comparable to that of the selected private qualified health plans (QHP), with some differences. In particular, the plans were generally comparable in that most covered the services GAO reviewed with the notable exceptions of pediatric dental and certain enabling services such as translation and transportation services, which were covered more frequently by the CHIP plans. For example, only the selected QHP in New York covered pediatric dental services; the QHPs in the other four states did not include pediatric dental services, although some officials indicated this would change for 2015 offerings. In those four states, stand-alone dental plans (SADP) could be purchased separately. Selected CHIP plans and QHPs were also similar in terms of the services on which they imposed day, visit, or dollar limits, although the five selected CHIP plans generally imposed fewer limits than the selected QHPs. For services where coverage limits were sometimes imposed on QHPs and CHIP plans, GAO's review found that the limits on CHIP plans were at times less restrictive. For example, the selected QHP in Utah limited home- and community-based health care services to 60 visits per year while the selected CHIP plan did not impose any limits. In addition, for pediatric dental services, coverage limits in the selected SADPs were generally similar to those in the selected CHIP plan; however, when there were differences, CHIP was generally more generous.

Consumers' costs for these services—defined as deductibles, copayments, coinsurance, and premiums—were almost always less in the five states' selected CHIP plans when compared to their respective QHPs, despite the application of subsidies authorized under the Patient Protection and Affordable Care Act (PPACA) that reduce these costs in the QHPs. Specifically, when cost-sharing applied, the amount was typically less for CHIP plans, even considering PPACA provisions aimed at reducing cost-sharing amounts for certain low income consumers who purchased QHPs. For example, an office visit to a specialist in Colorado would cost a CHIP enrollee a $2 to $10 copayment per visit, depending on their income, compared to the lowest available copayment of $25 per visit in the selected Colorado QHP. GAO's review of premium data further suggests that selected CHIP premiums were always lower than selected QHP premiums, even when considering the application of PPACA subsidies that help to defray the cost to certain consumers. For example, the 2014 annual premium for the selected Illinois CHIP plan for an individual at 150 percent of the federal poverty level (FPL) was $0. By comparison, the 2014 annual premium for the selected Illinois QHP was $1,254, which was reduced to $944 for an individual at 150 percent of the FPL, after considering federal subsidies to offset the cost of coverage. Finally, all selected CHIP plans and QHPs GAO reviewed limited out-of-pocket maximum costs, and these maximum costs were typically less in the CHIP plans.

ABBREVIATIONS

ASPE	Assistant Secretary for Planning and Evaluation
AV	actuarial value
CHIP	State Children's Health Insurance Program
CMS	Centers for Medicare & Medicaid Services
EHB	essential health benefits
EPSDT	Early and Periodic Screening, Diagnostic and Treatment
FPL	federal poverty level
HHS	Department of Health and Human Services
MAGI	Modified Adjusted Gross Income
PPACA	Patient Protection and Affordable Care Act
QHP	qualified health plan
SADP	stand-alone dental plan

February 25, 2015

The Honorable Orrin G. Hatch
Chairman
Committee on Finance
United States Senate

The Honorable Fred Upton
Chairman
Committee on Energy and Commerce
House of Representatives

Federal funding appropriated to states to support the State Children's Health Insurance Program (CHIP), a joint federal-state program that was established in 1997 to provide health coverage to certain low-income children, will end after September 2015 unless Congress acts to appropriate new funds. CHIP finances health insurance for over 8 million children whose household incomes are too high for Medicaid eligibility but may be too low to afford private insurance, and federal funds are expected to run out shortly after the end of fiscal year 2015.[1] Since January 2014, federal subsidies have been available to qualifying individuals to offset the cost of private health insurance purchased through health insurance exchanges—marketplaces where eligible individuals can compare and select among qualified health plans (QHP) and stand-alone dental plans (SADP) offered by participating private issuers—established under the Patient Protection and Affordable Care Act (PPACA).[2] PPACA also requires that, beginning in October 2015, if a state's CHIP funding is insufficient to cover all CHIP-eligible children, the state must establish procedures to ensure that the children who are not covered by CHIP are screened for Medicaid eligibility. If found ineligible for Medicaid, the children may be enrolled into a QHP that has been certified as comparable to CHIP by the Secretary of Health and Human Services (HHS), if such a QHP is available.[3]

States administer their CHIP programs under broad federal requirements, and programs vary in the services covered and the costs to individuals and families. For example, states can operate CHIP as a separate program, include CHIP-eligible children in their Medicaid program, or do both. [4] HHS' Centers for Medicare & Medicaid Services (CMS) is the federal agency responsible for overseeing CHIP.

In November 2013, we issued a report that compared coverage of services and costs to consumers in separate CHIP plans and plans intended as models for the benefits that would be offered through QHPs, known as benchmark plans, in five states—Colorado Kansas, Illinois, New York, and Utah—and described how coverage and costs might change in 2014.[5] We found that coverage in selected separate CHIP plans was generally comparable to benchmark plans and consumers' costs for these services were almost always less in CHIP than in benchmark plans. We also concluded that uncertainty remained regarding issuer decisions regarding how to define certain covered services and the implementation of other PPACA provisions, such as pediatric dental services, and that further study would be beneficial. At the time, QHPs were not available for study.

Now that QHPs have been made available on the exchanges, you asked us to examine the comparability of benefits and costs to consumers between CHIP plans and QHPs. In this report, we describe (1) how coverage of services in separate CHIP plans compares to QHPs in selected states, and (2) how costs to consumers in separate CHIP plans compare to QHPs in selected states.

To address both objectives, we selected the same health care services we reviewed in our 2013 report, which were identified by reviewing federal statutes and regulations governing CHIP-eligible services and the essential health benefit (EHB) categories, which are those 10 categories of service that QHPs are required to cover.[6] In addition to these services, we also identified selected enabling services, which can help individuals access the medical care they need and are recognized by the Health Resources and Services Administration's Maternal and Child Health Bureau as especially important for low income children and those with special health care needs, a significant number of whom rely on Medicaid or CHIP for some or all of their health care coverage.[7] We focused our review on the five states selected for our November 2013 report: Colorado, Kansas, Illinois, New York, and Utah, selected on the basis of variations in CMS region, CHIP program design, and size of enrollment in the separate CHIP program.[8] For these five states, we contacted state officials to identify the separate CHIP plan with the largest enrollment in 2014 and obtained plan coverage and cost sharing information from them for that CHIP plan in each state.

To compare the CHIP plan coverage and costs to that in QHPs, we identified the lowest cost silver level QHP in the most populous county in each of the five states in 2014 by reviewing 2010 Census data and information available on data.healthcare.gov for states with a federally facilitated exchange and from state officials in states operating their own exchanges.[9] We also relied on these data sources to identify the lowest cost SADP in 2014 in each state where the pediatric dental benefit was not included in our selected QHP. We then reviewed Evidences of Coverage from each of the QHPs and SADPs identified to determine whether the services we identified were covered; whether there were any annual limits on those services in terms of days, visits, age, or expenditures; and to identify cost-sharing amounts, including deductibles, copayments, and coinsurance, for each of the services and any stated out-of-pocket maximum costs.[10] We obtained 2014 CHIP premiums from state officials and 2014 QHP premiums from data.healthcare.gov, state websites, and state officials. We also obtained enrollment data for federally facilitated exchange states from HHS's Assistant Secretary for Planning and Evaluation (ASPE).[11] Finally, we interviewed state officials, including from CHIP programs and insurance departments in our five states, officials from an SADP issuer in one of our five states, and representatives from two large issuer associations whose members participate in both CHIP and the marketplaces to obtain their input on the implementation of certain PPACA provisions.

Our coverage and cost comparisons were limited to the selected services, limits, and plans in these five states, and our results cannot be generalized to other plans or states. To determine the reliability of the information from data.heathcare.gov, we spoke with researchers who have used these data to learn about any potential limitations. To determine the reliability of information from state officials regarding QHP identification and premiums, we interviewed officials regarding the steps they took to assess its reliability. To determine the reliability of enrollment data from ASPE, we interviewed officials regarding the steps they took to assess its reliability, and performed minimal data checks for obvious errors. We did not independently verify the accuracy or completeness of the data beyond these steps. Based on these efforts, we determined that these data sources were sufficiently reliable for the purposes of this report.

We conducted this performance audit from November 2014 to February 2015 in accordance with generally accepted government auditing standards. Those standards require that we plan and perform the audit to obtain sufficient, appropriate evidence to provide a reasonable basis for our findings and conclusions based on our audit objectives. We believe that the evidence obtained provides a reasonable basis for our findings and conclusions based on our audit objectives.

Background

Coverage and Cost Requirements for CHIP

Unlike states that opt to cover CHIP-eligible children in their Medicaid programs and therefore must extend Medicaid covered services to CHIP-eligible individuals, states with separate CHIP programs have flexibility in program design and are at liberty to modify certain aspects of their programs, such as coverage and cost-sharing requirements. However, federal laws and regulations require states' separate CHIP programs to include coverage for routine check-ups, immunizations, emergency services, and dental services defined as "necessary to prevent disease and promote oral health, restore oral structures to health and function, and treat emergency conditions." States typically cover a broad array of additional services in their separate CHIP programs and, in some states, adopt the Medicaid requirement to cover Early and Periodic Screening, Diagnostic and Treatment (EPSDT) services.[12] State CHIP programs must also comply with mental health parity requirements—meaning they must apply any financial requirements or limits on mental health or substance abuse benefits in the same manner as applied to medical and surgical benefits.

With respect to costs to consumers, CHIP premiums and cost-sharing—irrespective of program design—may not exceed amounts as defined by law. States may vary separate CHIP premiums and cost-sharing based on income and family size, as long as cost-sharing for higher-income children is not lower than for lower-income children. Federal laws and regulations also impose additional limits on premiums and cost-sharing for children in families with incomes at or below 150 percent of the federal poverty level (FPL). In all cases, no cost-sharing can be required for preventive services—defined as well-baby and well-child care, including age-appropriate immunizations and pregnancy-related services. In addition, states may not impose premiums and cost-sharing that, in the aggregate, exceed 5 percent of a family's total income for the length of the child's eligibility period in CHIP.[13]

Coverage and Cost Requirements for QHPs

PPACA includes provisions that seek to standardize coverage and costs of private health plans in the individual and small group markets. QHPs offered both on and off the exchanges are required to comply with applicable private insurance market reforms, including relevant premium rating requirements, the elimination of lifetime and annual dollar limits on EHBs, prohibition of cost-sharing for preventive services, mental health parity requirements, and the offering of comprehensive coverage. PPACA allows exchanges in each state to offer coverage of pediatric dental services as an integrated benefit in a QHP or through an SADP, which consumers can purchase separately. In exchanges with at least one participating SADP, QHPs are not required to include the pediatric dental benefit. Some states require children obtaining coverage in their state-based exchanges to enroll in an SADP if their QHP does not include the pediatric dental benefit; consumers purchasing coverage in the federally facilitated exchange are not required to do so.[14]

With respect to costs to consumers, QHPs must offer coverage that meets one of four metal tier levels, which correspond to actuarial value (AV) percentages that range from 60 to 90 percent: bronze (AV of 60 percent), silver (AV of 70 percent), gold (AV of 80 percent), or platinum (AV of 90 percent).[15] AV indicates the proportion of allowable charges that a health plan will pay, on average—the higher the AV, the lower the cost-sharing expected to be paid by consumers. Cost-sharing subsidies are available to individuals with incomes between 100 and 250 percent of the FPL to offset the costs they incur through copayments, coinsurance, and deductibles in a silver-level QHP. The cost-sharing subsidies are not provided directly to consumers; instead, QHP issuers are required to offer three variations of each silver plan they market through an exchange in the individual market. These plans are to reflect the cost-sharing subsidies through lower out-of-pocket maximum costs and, if necessary, through lower deductibles, copayments, or coinsurance. Once the adjustments from the subsidies are made, the AV of the silver plan available to eligible consumers will effectively increase from 70 percent to 73, 87, or 94 percent, depending on income. SADPs have different AV requirements than QHPs. SADPs are categorized as "high" and "low" level plans, with 85 and 70 percent AV, respectively.[16] Cost-sharing subsidies are not available for pediatric dental costs incurred by a consumer enrolled in an SADP.

PPACA also provides a premium tax credit to eligible individuals who purchase QHPs through the exchanges and who have incomes that are between 100 and 400 percent of the FPL. Depending on their income, this provision limits the amount families must contribute to QHP premiums to between 2 and 9.5 percent, inclusive, of their annual income; in 2014 these premium contributions ranged from $471 to $8,949 for a family of four. The premium tax credit is available to eligible consumers regardless of which metal tier they choose; however, the credit is calculated based on the second-lowest cost silver plan in the rating area in which the consumer resides.[17] Unlike cost-sharing subsidies, which generally do not apply to costs incurred for services by a consumer enrolled in an SADP, the maximum contribution amount on premiums includes premiums for both QHPs and SADPs, if relevant.[18]

Finally, PPACA established out-of-pocket maximum costs that apply to EHBs included in QHPs and SADPs. In 2014, these maximum costs for QHPs ranged from $2,250 to $6,350 for individuals and $4,500 to $12,700 for families for households with incomes between 100 and 400 percent of the FPL. Out-of-pocket maximum costs for SADPs are in addition to the out-of-pocket maximum costs for QHPs and were established by each exchange in 2014.

CHIP-Eligible Children and Enrollment in QHPs

CHIP-eligible children may enroll in QHPs instead of enrolling in CHIP—either through a child-only plan or through a plan with other family members—but they are ineligible for premium tax credits and cost-sharing subsidies because of their eligibility for CHIP. However, if a state experiences a CHIP funding shortfall in the future and is therefore unable to enroll all CHIP-eligible children into a CHIP plan, such children may qualify for premium tax credits and cost-sharing subsidies to offset the cost of QHP coverage.[19] In states not experiencing a funding shortfall, enrolling CHIP-eligible children in QHPs would generally increase costs for families. Under CMS regulations, if an individual who is ineligible for cost-sharing subsidies enrolls in the same policy as another family member who is eligible for cost-sharing subsidies, nobody covered under the policy will qualify for cost-sharing subsidies.[20] As a result, enrolling CHIP-eligible children in QHPs could result in a loss of cost-sharing subsidies for family members that are eligible for these subsidies. To maintain cost-sharing subsidies for eligible family members, the CHIP-eligible child would need to be enrolled in a child-only health plan, for which premium tax credits would be unavailable because of the child's eligibility for CHIP.

In Five States, Coverage in Selected CHIP Plans and QHPs Was Generally Comparable, Although the CHIP Plans More Commonly Covered Dental and Certain Enabling Services and Had Fewer Coverage Limits

We determined that coverage in the selected CHIP plans and QHPs in our five states was generally comparable in that it included some level of coverage for nearly all the services we reviewed.[21] Notable exceptions were certain enabling services and pediatric dental services, which were more frequently covered by the selected CHIP plans.[22] (See app. I for a detailed list of selected services covered by the plans we reviewed.) With respect to certain enabling services, which may be particularly important for low income children, care coordination or case management was offered by all selected CHIP plans, but by only one selected QHP. Similarly, routine transportation to and from medical appointments was covered by two CHIP plans but by none of the selected QHPs.[23] With respect to pediatric dental services, the QHP in New York was the only selected QHP that covered them; the selected QHPs in the other four states did not integrate pediatric dental services within the medical coverage they offered.[24] To obtain coverage for pediatric dental services, consumers who purchased the selected QHP in these states would also need to purchase an SADP. For consumers who purchased the selected QHP in New York or the selected SADP in the other four states, we determined that pediatric dental coverage available was generally comparable to what was available in their state's selected CHIP plan, with the exception of Utah, where the selected CHIP plan was more generous than the selected SADP.[25]

However, the extent to which consumers obtained coverage that included pediatric dental services is not clear. Available federal data with information on QHP enrollment suggest that many children in the United States with exchange coverage in 2014 may have been without comprehensive dental coverage. According to our analysis of enrollment data for 2014 provided by ASPE, 16 percent of children younger than 18 years of age in the 36 states with federally facilitated exchanges were enrolled in a QHP that included comprehensive dental services that covered check-ups, basic, and major dental services.[26] The remaining children were enrolled in QHPs that either had less than comprehensive or no dental coverage. Some of these families are likely to have purchased an SADP for their children, however. According to an ASPE report issued in May 2014, 18 percent of children younger than 18 years of age in the 36 states with federally facilitated exchanges who enrolled in a QHP also enrolled in an SADP, and these were likely among the families that had no comprehensive dental coverage included in their QHP.[27] According to our analysis of enrollment data for 2014 provided by ASPE, virtually no children younger than 18 years of age in the 36 states with federally facilitated exchanges were enrolled in a QHP that included comprehensive dental services and an SADP.

Selected CHIP plans and QHPs were also similar in terms of the services on which they imposed day, visit, or dollar limits; however, in the aggregate, CHIP plans imposed fewer limits than QHPs. (See fig.1.) The selected CHIP plans and QHPs we reviewed were generally similar in that they typically did not impose day, visit, or dollar limits on office visits, emergency care, prescription drugs, and preventive care, but commonly did impose limits on outpatient therapies, pediatric vision, and pediatric hearing. One notable difference between these selected CHIP plans and QHPs was the frequency by which they limited home-and community-based health care. While the selected QHP in four states imposed day or visit limits on these services, only one state's selected CHIP plan did so. In contrast, no QHPs imposed limits on durable medical equipment, while one CHIP plan imposed a $2,000 annual limit.

For services where coverage limits were sometimes imposed on QHPs and CHIP plans, our review found that the limits on CHIP plans were at times less restrictive. For example, the selected QHP in Utah limited home- and community-based health care services to 60 visits per year while the selected CHIP plan in the state did not impose any limits on these services. Comparability between service limits in states' selected CHIP plans and QHPs was less clear for outpatient therapy services. For example, the selected CHIP plan in New York limited outpatient physical and occupational therapies to 6 weeks per year, with no limits on outpatient speech therapy, while the selected QHP in the state limited outpatient therapies to a combined 60 visits per condition per lifetime. (See app. II for a detailed list of coverage limits for services we reviewed in the selected plans.)

In addition, for pediatric dental services, coverage limits in the selected QHP and SADPs were generally similar to those in the selected CHIP plan; however, when there were differences, CHIP was generally more generous. For example, the selected CHIP plan in Kansas allowed one sealant per tooth per year; in contrast, the selected high and low SADP in the state allowed one sealant per tooth every three years.

Similarly, the selected CHIP plan in Utah did not have any coverage limits on x-rays while the selected high and low SADPs in the state did. (See app. III for a detailed list of selected dental limits we reviewed in selected plans.)

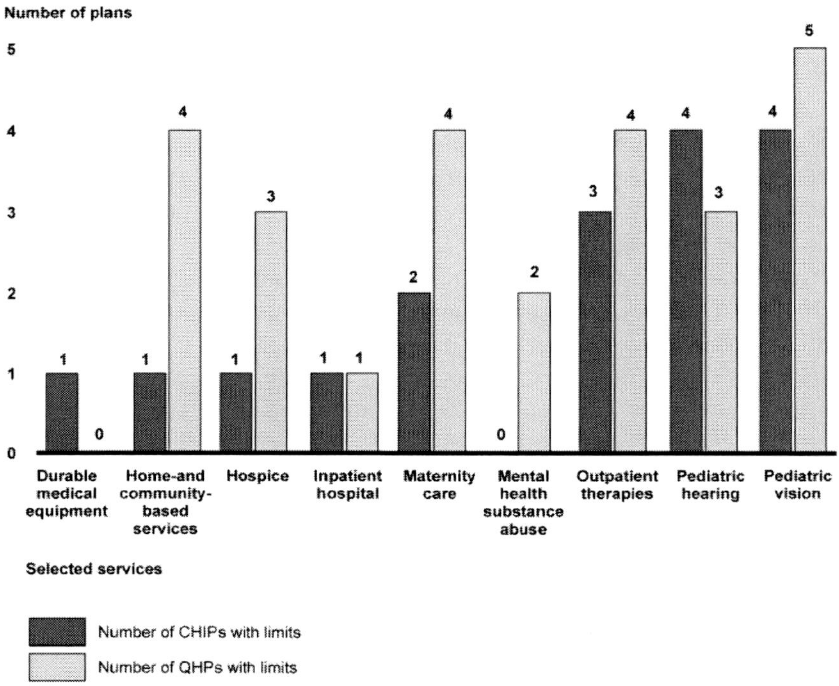

Source: GAO analysis of information from states and QHPs. | GAO-15-323.

Note: We did not identify any limits on the following services in the selected CHIP plans and QHPs: office visits, emergency care, prescription drugs, preventive services, and when covered, enabling services. Coverage limits on pediatric dental services are excluded from this table because the selected QHP in four of the five states did not cover pediatric dental services.

Figure 1. Selected Services with Coverage Limits in State Children's Health Insurance Program (CHIP) Plans and Qualified Health Plans (QHP) GAO Reviewed in Five States, Calendar Year 2014.

COSTS TO CONSUMERS WERE ALMOST ALWAYS LESS IN SELECTED CHIP PLANS THAN IN SELECTED QHPS DESPITE PPACA PROVISIONS THAT LIMIT QHP COSTS

We determined that costs to consumers were almost always less in the selected CHIP plans than in the selected QHPs. Even considering PPACA provisions aimed at reducing cost-sharing amounts for certain low-income consumers who purchased QHPs, the differences remained, though were smaller. For example, the selected CHIP plans in four of the five states did not include any deductible, which means that enrollees in those states did not need to pay a specified amount before the plan began paying for services.[28] In contrast, QHPs we reviewed typically imposed annual deductibles, which were as high as $500 for an individual and $1,500 for a family in the plan variation that offered the lowest available deductibles for QHP enrollees.[29] In addition, consumers who purchase selected SADPs may face separate deductible costs. For example, whereas dental services were subject to the plan deductible in the New York QHP, SADPs in Colorado, Illinois, and Kansas had separate dental deductibles that ranged from $25 to $50 for individuals enrolled in selected high plans to $45 to $50 for individuals enrolled in selected low plans. (See app. III for a detailed list of selected dental cost-sharing we reviewed in the selected plans.)

For services we reviewed where the plans imposed copayments or coinsurance, the amount was typically less in a state's selected CHIP plan compared to its selected QHP, even considering PPACA provisions aimed at reducing cost-sharing amounts for certain low income consumers who purchased QHPs.[30] For example, the selected CHIP plan in two of our five states – Kansas and New York – did not impose copayments or coinsurance on any of the services we reviewed. In two of the remaining three states, the selected CHIP plan imposed copayments or coinsurance on less than half of the services we reviewed, and the amounts were usually minimal and on a sliding income scale.[31] For example, for each brand-name prescription drug, the Illinois CHIP plan imposed a $3.90 copayment on enrollees with incomes greater than 142 and up to 157 percent of the FPL, which was increased to $7 for enrollees with incomes greater than 209 and up to 313 percent of the FPL. In contrast, selected QHPs in all five states imposed copayments or coinsurance on most covered services we reviewed, and the amounts were consistently higher than the CHIP plan in the same state. For example, depending on income, the copayment for primary care and specialist physician visits in Colorado ranged from $2 to $10 per visit for enrollees in the selected CHIP plan, but was $25 and $35 per visit, respectively, for all enrollees in the selected QHP. Cost-sharing for dental services was also higher in a state's selected SADP than in its selected CHIP plan a majority of the time. In addition, in states where the selected QHP charged coinsurance and the selected CHIP plan required a copayment, a direct comparison of cost differences could not be made, although data suggest CHIP costs would generally be lower. For example, for an inpatient hospital admission, higher-income enrollees in the selected CHIP plan in Colorado paid $50, while all enrollees in the selected QHP in the state were responsible for 20 percent coinsurance after the deductible was met, an amount that was likely to be higher given that 20 percent of the average price for an inpatient facility stay in 2011 was over $3,000.[32] (See app. IV for a detailed list of cost-sharing for services we reviewed in selected plans.)

Our review of premiums for selected CHIP plans and QHPs also suggests that premiums were always less in the CHIP plans than in the QHPs we reviewed, even with the application of the premium tax credit to defray the cost of QHP premiums. For example, according to CHIP officials, annual CHIP premiums in 2014 for an individual varied by income level and ranged from $0 for the lowest income CHIP enrollees in Colorado, Illinois, Kansas, and New York, to $720 for enrollees between 351 and 400 percent of the FPL in New York, with most enrollees across the five selected states paying less than $200 per year.[33] By comparison, 2014 annual premiums for a single child only enrolled in selected QHPs ranged from $1,111 to $1,776 in our five states before the application of the premium tax credit. With the premium tax credit, the annual premium amount for selected QHPs was often significantly lower, but was still higher than the selected CHIP plan in all five states. For example, in Illinois, the premium for the selected CHIP plan for an individual with an income at 150 percent of the FPL was $0 and was $1,254 for the selected QHP, which was reduced to $944 after the premium tax credit was applied.

However, the additional premium cost to families enrolling previously eligible CHIP children into their QHPs—a possibility if CHIP funding is not reauthorized—may be minimal or nothing. 34 Because PPACA limits the amount lower income families pay in premiums, families with incomes at 250 percent or less of the FPL—at least 75 percent of the separate CHIP enrollees in the states we reviewed—would generally pay no additional premium to add a child to their QHP. For example, in Kansas, the 2014 annual premium for the lowest cost silver level QHP was $4,875 for a couple age 40 and an additional $1,211 to add a child. However, if the couple's income was 200 percent of the

FPL, their maximum annual premium would be $2,494, and they would incur no additional costs by adding a child to their plan.[35]

Finally, all selected CHIP plans and QHPs limited the total potential costs to consumers by imposing out-of-pocket maximum costs, and these maximum costs were typically less in the CHIP plans we reviewed. For example, all five states applied the limit a family could pay in CHIP plans as established under federal law—including deductibles, copayments, coinsurance, and premiums—at 5 percent of a family's income during the child's (or children's) eligibility for CHIP. This 5 percent cap resulted in limits that varied based on a family's income level. This amount ranged from $584 to $2,334 for individuals, and $1,193 to $4,770 for a family of four, between 100 and 400 percent of the FPL in 2014. PPACA also established out-of-pocket maximum costs that apply to QHPs and may vary by income.[36] Unlike CHIP, however, QHP maximums do not include premiums, which may be separately reduced through the application of premium tax credits. QHPs may set out-of-pocket maximum costs that are lower than those established by PPACA, which was the case for three of the five selected QHPs.[37] For example, the selected QHP in Colorado had individual out-of-pocket maximum costs ranging from $750 to $6,300 for individuals between 100 and 400 percent FPL. This amount was less than out-of-pocket maximum costs established under federal law, which ranged from $2,250 to $6,350 for individuals between 100 and 400 percent FPL in 2014.

Out-of-pocket maximum costs for SADPs are in addition to the out-of-pocket maximum costs for QHPs and may increase potential costs for families who purchase them. In 2014, each exchange established maximum out-of-pocket costs for SADPs, which do not include premiums. Annual out-of-pocket maximum costs for selected SADPs for three of the four selected SADPs were $700 for one child and $1400 for two or more children.[38]

AGENCY COMMENTS

We provided a draft of this report for comment to HHS. HHS officials provided technical comments, which we incorporated as appropriate.

Katherine M. Iritani
Director, Health Care

Appendix I: Coverage for Selected Services in CHIP Plans and Qualified Health Plans (QHP) GAO Reviewed in Five States

Service			CO	IL	KS	NY	UT		CO	IL	KS	NY	UT
Ambulatory patient services	Provider office visits		✓	✓	✓	✓	✓		✓	✓	✓	✓	✓
Outpatient surgery			✓	✓	✓	✓	✓		✓	✓	✓	✓	✓
Emergency care			✓	✓	✓	✓	✓		✓	✓	✓	✓	✓
Inpatient hospital	Facility		✓	✓	✓	✓	✓		✓	✓	✓	✓	✓
	Professional		✓	✓	✓	✓	✓		✓	✓	✓	✓	✓
	Ancillary		✓	✓	✓	✓	✓		✓	✓	✓	✓	✓
Maternity care			✓	✓	✓	✓	✓		✓	✓	✓	✓	✓
Mental health	Inpatient		✓	✓	✓	✓	✓		✓	✓	✓	✓	✓
	Outpatient		✓	✓	✓	✓	✓		✓	✓	✓	✓	✓
Substance abuse	Inpatient		✓	✓	✓	✓	✓		✓	✓	✓	✓	✓
	Outpatient		✓	✓	✓	✓	✓		✓	✓	✓	✓	✓
Prescription drugs			✓	✓	✓	✓	✓		✓	✓	✓	✓	✓
Outpatient therapies	Physical	Rehabilitative	✓	✓	✓	✓	✓		✓	✓	✓	✓	✓
		Habilitative	✓	✓	☒	✓	✓		✓	✓	✓	✓	✓
	Speech	Rehabilitative	✓	✓	✓	✓	✓		✓	✓	✓	✓	✓

Service			CO	IL	KS	NY	UT		CO	IL	KS	NY	UT
		Habilitative	✓	✓	☒	✓	✓		✓	✓	✓	✓	✓
	Occupational	Rehabilitative	✓	✓	✓	✓	✓		✓	✓	✓	✓	✓
		Habilitative	✓	✓	☒	✓	✓		✓	✓	✓	✓	✓
Laboratory services	Inpatient		✓	✓	✓	✓	✓		✓	✓	✓	✓	✓
	Outpatient		✓	✓	✓	✓	✓		✓	✓	✓	✓	✓
Preventive care	Well-child		✓	✓	✓	✓	✓		✓	✓	✓	✓	✓
	Immunizations		✓	✓	✓	✓	✓		✓	✓	✓	✓	✓
	Chronic disease management		✓	✓	✓	✓	✓		✓	✓	✓	✓	✓
Pediatric dental	Routine		✓	✓	✓	✓	✓		☒	☒	☒	✓	☒
	Emergency		✓	✓	✓	✓	✓		✓	✓	✓	✓	✓
	Other		✓	✓	✓	✓	✓		☒	☒	☒	✓	☒
Pediatric vision	Exams		✓	✓	✓	✓	✓		✓	✓	✓	✓	✓
	Corrective lenses		✓	✓	✓	✓	☒		✓	✓	✓	✓	☒
Pediatric hearing	Testing (screening and/or exam)		✓	✓	✓	✓	✓		✓	✓	✓	✓	✓
	Hearing aids		✓	✓	✓	✓	☒		✓	✓	✓[a]	✓	☒

Appendix I. (Continued)

Service		CO	IL	KS	NY	UT		CO	IL	KS	NY	UT
Durable medical equipment		✓	✓	✓	✓	✓		✓	✓	✓	✓	✓
Home- and community-based health care		✓	✓	✓	✓	✓		✓	✓	✓	✓	✓
Hospice		✓	✓	✓	✓	✓		✓	✓	✓	✓	✓
Enabling services	Non-hospice respite care	☒	☒	✓	☒	☒		☒	☒	☒	☒	☒
	Translation during office visits	✓	☒	✓	✓	✓		☒	☒	☒	☒	☒
	Care coordination/case management	✓	✓	✓	✓	✓[b]		☒	✓	☒	☒	☒
	Routine transportation[c]	☒	✓[d]	✓	☒	☒		☒	☒	☒	☒	☒

Legend: ✓= yes; ☒ = no.

Source: GAO analysis of information from states and QHPs. | GAO-15-323

Notes: CHIP plan information was provided by state officials for the Colorado Access CHIP plan, Illinois CHIP and Medicaid State plans, Kansas Sunflower State Health CHIP plan, Fidelis Care New York CHIP plan, and Utah CHIP Select Health plan. QHP information is from Evidences of Coverage for the Colorado Humana Connect Silver 4600/6300 plan, Illinois Blue Choice Silver PPO 003 plan, Kansas Coventry Health and Life Silver Integrated $10 Copay PPO KC Exchange plan, New York MetroPlus SilverPlus S1 plan, and the Utah Humana Connect Silver 4600/6300 plan, and state and QHP officials.

The Patient Protection and Affordable Care Act (PPACA) allows exchanges in each state to make available coverage of pediatric dental services as an embedded benefit in a QHP or through a standalone dental plan (SADP), which consumers may purchase separately.

In exchanges with at least one participating SADP, QHPs were not required to include the pediatric dental benefit. Consumers in these five states were not required to purchase SADPs in 2014, even if their QHP did not include the pediatric dental benefit.

Rehabilitation is provided to help a person regain, maintain or prevent deterioration of a skill that has been acquired but then lost or impaired due to illness, injury, or disabling condition. While PPACA and its implementing regulations do not define habilitative services, habilitation has been defined by several advocacy groups as a service that is provided in order for a person to attain, maintain, or prevent deterioration of a skill or function never learned or acquired due to a disabling condition.

[a]The plan covers bone anchored hearing aids and cochlear implants only. Bone anchored hearing aids are used when traditional hearing aids are not efficient because of complications such as chronic infections or blockage. Cochlear implants are for patients with severe hearing loss where traditional amplification is no longer beneficial.

[b]The plan covers care coordination and case management for children with special health care needs only. Utah CHIP defines children with special health care needs as enrollees who have or are at increased risk for chronic physical, developmental, behavioral, or emotional conditions and who also require health and related services of a type or amount beyond that required by adults and children generally.

[c]Routine transportation includes transportation to and from medical appointments.

[d]Routine transportation is covered for CHIP children greater than 142 and up to 209 percent of the federal poverty level only.

APPENDIX II: COVERAGE LIMITS FOR SELECTED SERVICES IN CHIP PLANS AND QHPS GAO REVIEWED IN FIVE STATES

Tables 1 and 2 provide information on coverage limits for selected services in State Children's Health Insurance Program (CHIP) plans and qualified health plans (QHP) in each of the five states we reviewed: Colorado, Illinois, Kansas, New York, and Utah. For coverage limits on pediatric dental services, see Appendix III.

Table 1. Annual Coverage Limits for Selected Services in State Children's Health Insurance Program (CHIP) Plans GAO Reviewed in Five States, Calendar Year 2014

					CHIP plan	
Service		**CO**	**IL**	**KS**	**NY**	**UT**
Ambulatory patient services: office visits	Primary care physician	None	None	None	None	None
	Specialty physician	None	None	None	None	None
Emergency care		None	None	None	None	None
Inpatient hospital		30 days for rehabilitation therapies[a]	None	None	None	None
Maternity care		1 metabolic screening, 1 postpartum visit, and 1 prescreening visit	None	None	1 home care visit for early discharge	None
Mental health and substance abuse	Inpatient	None	None	None	None	None
	Outpatient	None	None	None	None	None
Prescription drugs		None	None	None	None	None
Outpatient therapies (occupational, physical, speech)	Rehabilitative	30 visits[b]	None	None	Physical and occupational: 6 weeks; speech: none	20 visits per therapy type peryear
	Habilitative	30 visits[b]	None	Not covered	Physical and occupational: 6 weeks; speech: none	20 visits per therapy type peryear

					CHIP plan	
Service		**CO**	**IL**	**KS**	**NY**	**UT**
Preventive care		None	None	None	None	None
Pediatric vision	Optometrist exam	1 exam	None	None	1 exam[c]	1 exam
	Corrective lenses	$50	None	4 pair contacts	1 pair[d]	Not covered
Pediatric hearing	Testing	None	None	None	1 test	1 test
	Hearing aids	1 aid every 5 years	None	Various[e]	None	Not covered[f]
Durable medical equipment		$2,000	None	None	None	None
Home- and community-based health care		None	None	None	40 visits	None
Hospice		9 months[g]	None	None	None	None
Enabling services	Non-hospice respite care	Not covered	Not covered	None	Not covered	Not covered
	Translation services—office visits	None	Not covered	None	None	None
	Care coordination/case management	None	None	None	None	None
	Routine transportation[h]	Not covered	None	None	Not covered	Not covered

Source: GAO analysis of information from states. | GAO-15-323

Notes: CHIP plan information was provided by state officials for the Colorado Access CHIP plan, Illinois CHIP and Medicaid State plans, Kansas Sunflower State Health CHIP plan, Fidelis Care New York CHIP plan, and Utah CHIP Select Health plan.

Rehabilitation is provided to help a person regain, maintain or prevent deterioration of a skill that has been acquired but then lost or impaired due to illness, injury, or disabling condition. While federal law does not define habilitative services, habilitation has been defined by several advocacy groups as a service that is provided in order for a person to attain, maintain, or prevent deterioration of a skill or function never learned or acquired due to a disabling condition.

[a]Rehabilitation therapies are occupational, physical, and speech therapies.

[b]Outpatient therapy visit limits are per diagnosis, per calendar year. Service is unlimited to children under 3 years of age and speech therapy is unlimited for those with a cleft palate or lip.

[c]Optometrist exams are limited to one per year, unless they are required more frequently and the enrollee has the appropriate documentation.

[d]Enrollees are limited to one frame and one set of lenses per year, unless they are required more frequently and the enrollee has the appropriate documentation.

[e]Hearing aid batteries are limited to 6 batteries per month for monaural aids and 12 per month for binaural aids. Batteries for use with cochlear devices are limited to lithium ion (3 per 30 days) or zinc air (6 per 30 days). Batteries for cochlear devices are covered for CHIP-eligible beneficiaries only. Only one type of battery is allowed every 30 days.

[f]Hearing aids are not covered by CHIP unless following cochlear implants. [g]Hospice is available in 3 month increments, which do not have to be consecutive.

[h]Routine transportation includes transportation to and from medical appointments.

Table 2. Annual Coverage Limits for Selected Services in Qualified Health Plans (QHP) GAO Reviewed in Five States, Calendar Year 2014

		QHP				
Service		**CO**	**IL**	**KS**	**NY**	**UT**
Ambulatory patient services: office visits	Primary care physician	None	None	None	None	None
	Specialty physician	None	None	None	None	None
Emergency care		None	None	None	None	None
Inpatient hospital		None	None	None	Rehabilitation: 1 consecutive 60 day period per condition, per lifetime	None
Maternity care		1 home care visit for early discharge	1 inpatient newborn exam and hearing screening	None	1 home care visit for early discharge	1 home carevisit for earlydischarge
Mental health and substance abuse	Inpatient	None	None	None	None	None
	Outpatient	None	None	Partial day programs: 20 visits[a]	20 visits for family counseling (substance abuse only)	None
Prescription drugs		None	None	None	None	None

Table 2. (Continued)

		QHP				
Service		**CO**	**IL**	**KS**	**NY**	**UT**
Outpatient therapies (occupational, physical, speech)	Rehabilitative	20 visits per therapy	None	20 visits per therapy[b]	60 visits per condition, per lifetime, all therapies combined	20 visits per therapy type per year[c]
	Habilitative	20 visits per therapy[d]	None		60 visits per condition, per lifetime, all therapies combined	
Preventive care		None	None	None	None	None
Pediatric vision	Optometrist exam	1 exam	1 exam	None	1 exam	1 exam
	Corrective lenses	1 pair lenses; 1 frame every 2 years	1 pair lenses and frames or contacts	3 lenses or contacts; 3 frames	1 pair lenses and frames	Not covered
Pediatric hearing	Testing	None	None	None	None	None
	Hearing aids	1 aid every 5 years[e]	2 every 3 years	None[f]	Hearing aid: 1 every 3 years; cochlear implant and bone anchored: 1 per ear per time covered	Not covered

		QHP				
Service		**CO**	**IL**	**KS**	**NY**	**UT**
Durable medical equipment		None	None	None	None	None
Home- and community-based health care		7 visits per week	None	3 home care education visits	40 visits per year	60 visits per year
Hospice		None	None	Inpatient: 15 days	210 days	Part-time nursing and home health aide care: 8 hours a dayeach
Enabling services	Non-hospice respite care	Not covered	Not covered	Not covered	Not covered	Not covered
	Translation services—office visits	Not covered	Not covered	None	Not covered	None
	Care coordination/case management	Not covered	None	Not covered	Not covered	Not covered
	Routine transportation[g]	Not covered	Not covered	Not covered	Not covered	Not covered

Source: GAO analysis of information from states and QHPs. | GAO-15-323

Notes: QHP information is from Evidences of Coverage for the Colorado Humana Connect Silver 4600/6300 plan, Illinois Blue Choice Silver PPO 003 plan, Kansas Coventry Health and Life Silver Integrated $10 Copay PPO KC Exchange plan, New York MetroPlus SilverPlus S1 plan, and the Utah Humana Connect Silver 4600/6300 plan, and state and QHP officials.

Rehabilitation is provided to help a person regain, maintain or prevent deterioration of a skill that has been acquired but then lost or impaired due to illness, injury, or disabling condition. While federal law does not define habilitative services, habilitation has been defined by several advocacy groups as a service that is provided in order for a person to attain, maintain, or prevent deterioration of a skill or function never learned or acquired due to a disabling condition.

[a] A partial day program is any program 4 hours or longer per day.

[b]There is a combined visit limit for rehabilitative and habilitative physical, occupational, and speech therapies per therapy type.

[c]There is a combined visit limit for all rehabilitative and habilitative physical, occupational, and speech therapies.

[d]Habilitative outpatient therapies for treatment of congenital defects and birth abnormalities for a covered dependent are covered from a child's third to sixth birthday only.

[e]There are no limits if the existing hearing aid can't be altered to adequately meet the needs of the child.

[f]There are no coverage limits for bone-anchored hearing aids and cochlear implants, which are the only types of hearing aids covered by the plan.

[g]Routine transportation includes transportation to and from medical appointments.

Appendix III: Coverage, Coverage Limits, and Cost-Sharing for Selected Dental Services in CHIP Plans, QHPs, and SADPs

Tables 3 through 12 provide information on coverage, coverage limits, and cost-sharing—deductibles, copayments, and coinsurance—for selected dental services in State Children's Health Insurance Program (CHIP) plans we reviewed in five states: Colorado, Illinois, Kansas, New York, and Utah; a qualified health plan (QHP) in New York; and standalone dental plans (SADP) in Colorado, Illinois, Kansas, and Utah. For selected CHIP plans and the QHP in New York, we note differences in cost-sharing amounts by income level.[1] For selected SADPs, we note the cost-sharing amounts for the "high" and "low" level options, which have actuarial values of 85 and 70 percent, respectively.

For all five states, cost-sharing amounts were subject to out-of-pocket maximum costs. For CHIP enrollees in each state, cost-sharing and premium amounts were subject to a federally established out-of-pocket-maximum cost equal to 5 percent of a family's income. For QHP enrollees, issuers established an out-of-pocket maximum cost for each plan that was equal to or less than the out-of-pocket maximum cost established under the Patient Protection and Affordable Care Act (PPACA). PPACA out-of-pocket maximum costs for households with incomes between 100 and 400 percent of the federal poverty level (FPL) in 2014 ranged from $2,250 to $6,350 for individuals and $4,500 to $12,700 for families. In 2014, each exchange established out-of-pocket maximum costs for SADPs. Annual out-of-pocket maximum costs for the selected SADPs in Colorado, Illinois, and Kansas were $700 for one child and $1400 for two or more children. The selected SADP in Utah imposed an out-of-pocket maximum cost of $40 for the low plan and $20 for the high plan. In contrast to CHIP, the out-of-pocket maximum costs for QHPs and SADPs do not include premiums.

Table 3. Coverage and Coverage Limits for Selected Dental Services in the State Children's Health Insurance Program (CHIP) Plan and Stand-alone Dental Plan (SADP) GAO Reviewed in Colorado, Calendar Year 2014

		CHIP plan		High SADP		Low SADP	
Service		**Covered**	**Limits**	**Covered**	**Limits**	**Covered**	**Limits**
Routine	Periodic oral exam	Y	2 per year	Y	2 per year	Y	2 per year
	Cleaning	Y	2 per year	Y	2 per year	Y	1 per year
	X-rays[a]	Y	• Complete or panoramic: 1 every 5 years • Bitewings: 1 per year	Y	• Complete: 1 every 5 years • Bitewings: 1 per year	Y	• Complete and bitewings: 1 every 5 years • Bitewings: 1 per year • Panoramic: 1 every 5 years
	Fluoride treatment (gel or foam)	Y	2 per year	Y	2 per year, covered to age 19	Y	2 per year
	Sealants[b]	Y	1 every 3 years	Y	None, covered to age 19	Y	1 every 3 years; permanent molarsonly
	Space maintainers[c]	Y	None	Y	None, covered to age 19	Y	None
Other	Fillings	Y	1 every 2 years per tooth	Y	1 every 2 years per tooth	Y	1 every 2 years per tooth

		CHIP plan		High SADP		Low SADP	
Service		**Covered**	**Limits**	**Covered**	**Limits**	**Covered**	**Limits**
	Crowns[d]	Y	1 prefabricated every 2 years per tooth	Y	None, covered to age 19	Y	1 prefabricated every 2 years
	Root canals	Y	None	Y	1 per tooth	Y	None, permanent teeth only
	Dentures	Y	1 every 5 years, not covered < 16 years of age	Y	1 every 5 years, not covered < 16 years of age	N	Not covered

Source: GAO analysis of information from the state and SADPs. | GAO-15-323

Notes: CHIP plan information was provided by state officials. SADP information is from Evidences of Coverage for the Colorado Anthem Dental Pediatric (low SADP) and Delta Dental Family Plan – Mesa (high SADP) and state officials.

SADPs are categorized as "high" and "low" level plans, with 85 and 70 percent actuarial value (AV), respectively. AV indicates the proportion of allowable charges that a health plan will pay, on average—the higher the AV, the lower the cost-sharing expected to be paid by consumers.

[a]Complete x-rays cover the entire mouth. Panoramic x-rays show the entire mouth area on a single x-ray. Bitewings show details of the upper and lower teeth in one area of the mouth.

[b] A sealant is a thin, clear or white resin substance that is applied to the biting surfaces of teeth to prevent decay.

[c] A space maintainer is an appliance for a child that keeps space open to allow a permanent tooth to erupt and come into place. The selected CHIP plans and SADPs cover space maintainers for the premature loss of baby back teeth only.

[d] Prefabricated crowns are used on permanent teeth primarily as a temporary measure. For children, prefabricated crowns are commonly used on primary, or baby, teeth.

Table 4. Coverage and Coverage Limits for Selected Dental Services in the State Children's Health Insurance Program (CHIP) Plan and Stand-alone Dental Plan (SADP) GAO Reviewed in Illinois, Calendar Year 2014

			CHIP plan		High SADP		Low SADP
Service		Covered	Limits	Covered	Limits	Covered	Limits
Routine	Periodic oral exam	Y	2 per year[a]	Y	2 per year	Y	2 per year
	Cleaning	Y	2 per year[b]	Y	2 per year	Y	2 per year
	X-rays[c]	Y	• Complete, panoramic, or vertical bitewings: 1 every 3 years •Bitewings: 1 per year	Y	• Complete or panoramic: 1 every 3 years • Bitewings: 1 per year	Y	• Complete or panoramic: 1 every 3 years • Bitewings: 1 per year
	Fluoride treatment (gel or foam)	Y	• 1 per year age 3-20[d] • 3 per year age 0-2[d]	Y	1 per year	Y	1 per year
	Sealants[e]	Y	1 per tooth per lifetime[f]	Y	1 per tooth per lifetime	Y	1 per tooth per lifetime
	Space maintainers[g]	Y	• 1 per quadrant per lifetime (4) •1 per arch per lifetime (2)	Y	• 1 per quadrant per lifetime (4) •1 per arch per lifetime (2)	Y	• 1 per quadrant per lifetime (4) •1 per arch per lifetime (2)

			CHIP plan		High SADP		Low SADP
Service		Covered	Limits	Covered	Limits	Covered	Limits
Other	Fillings	Y	1 per tooth surface per year	Y	1 per tooth surface per year	Y	1 per tooth surface per year
	Crowns[h]	Y	•1 permanent every 5 years •1 prefabricated per tooth per lifetime (primary and anterior) •1 prefabricated per tooth every 5 years (permanent)	Y	•1 permanent every 5 years •1 prefabricated per tooth per lifetime (1 every 5 years for primary teeth)	Y	•1 permanent every 5 years •1 prefabricatedper tooth per lifetime (1 every 5 years for primary teeth)
	Root canals	Y	1 per tooth per lifetime	Y	1 per tooth per lifetime	Y	1 per tooth per lifetime
	Dentures	Y	1 every 5 years	Y	1 every 5 years	Y	1 every 5 years

Source: GAO analysis of information from the state and SADP. | GAO-15-323

Notes: CHIP plan information was provided by state officials. SADP information is from Evidences of Coverage for the Illinois Dentegra Dental PPO Children's 70 (low SADP) and 85 (high SADP) plan and state and SADP officials.

SADPs are categorized as "high" and "low" level plans, with 85 and 70 percent actuarial value (AV), respectively. AV indicates the proportion of allowable charges that a health plan will pay, on average—the higher the AV, the lower the cost-sharing expected to be paid by consumers.

[a]The Illinois CHIP plan also covers one cleaning per year at a school that is at least 270 days from the last school exam. The benefit limitations for these services are unique based upon the place of service, school or office.

[b]The Illinois CHIP plan also covers 2 cleanings per year at a school. The benefit limitations for these services are unique based upon the place of service, school or office.

[c]Complete x-rays cover the entire mouth. Panoramic x-rays show the entire mouth area on a single x-ray. Bitewings show details of the upper and lower teeth in one area of the mouth.

[d]The Illinois CHIP plan also covers 1 fluoride treatment per year at a school. The benefit limitations for these services are unique based upon the place of service, school or office.

[e]A sealant is a thin, clear or white resin substance that is applied to the biting surfaces of teeth to prevent decay.

[f]Sealants are covered for the following teeth: 2, 3, 14, 15, 18, 19, 30, and 31.

[g]A space maintainer is an appliance for a child that keeps space open to allow a permanent tooth to erupt and come into place. The mouth has four quadrants and two arches.

[h]Prefabricated crowns are used on permanent teeth primarily as a temporary measure. For children, prefabricated crowns are commonly used on primary, or baby, teeth.

Table 5. Coverage and Coverage Limits for Selected Dental Services in the State Children's Health Insurance Program (CHIP) Plan and Stand-alone Dental Plan (SADP) GAO Reviewed in Kansas, Calendar Year 2014

		CHIP plan		**High SADP**		**Low SADP**	
Service		**Covered**	**Limits**	**Covered**	**Limits**	**Covered**	**Limits**
Routine	Periodic oral exam	Y	2 per year	Y	2 per year	Y	2 per year
	Cleaning	Y	2 per year	Y	2 per year	Y	2 per year
	X-rays[a]	Y	Complete or panoramic and bitewings: 1 every 3 years	Y	• Complete or panoramic: 1 every 5 years •Bitewings: 2 per year	Y	• Complete or panoramic: 1 every 5 years •Bitewings: 2 per year

		CHIP plan		High SADP		Low SADP	
Service		**Covered**	**Limits**	**Covered**	**Limits**	**Covered**	**Limits**
	Fluoride treatment (gel or foam)	Y	3 per year	Y	2 per year	Y	2 per year
	Sealants[b]	Y	1 per tooth per year	Y	1 every 3 years[c]	Y	1 every 3 yearsc
	Space maintainers[d]	Y	1 per quadrant per year (4) 1 per arch per year (2)	Y	None[e]	Y	None[e]
Other	Fillings	Y	1 per year	Y	None	Y	None
	Crowns[f]	Y	•1 permanent every 5 years •1 prefabricated every 2 years	Y	•1 permanent every 5 years •1 prefabricated per tooth every 5 years for children less than 15 years of age	Y	•1 permanent every 5 years •1 prefabricatedper tooth every5 years for children less than 15 years of age
	Root canals	Y	1 per tooth per lifetime	Y	None	Y	None
	Dentures	Y	1 every 5 years	Y	1 every 5 years	Y	1 every 5 years

Source: GAO analysis of information from the state and SADP. | GAO-15-323

Notes: CHIP plan information was provided by state officials. SADP information is from Evidences of Coverage for the Kansas Best One Dental Basic- Silver (low SADP) and Best Life Best One Dental Plus- Gold (high SADP).

SADPs are categorized as "high" and "low" level plans, with 85 and 70 percent actuarial value (AV), respectively. AV indicates the proportion of allowable charges that a health plan will pay, on average—the higher the AV, the lower the cost-sharing expected to be paid by consumers.

[a]Complete x-rays cover the entire mouth. Panoramic x-rays show the entire mouth area on a single x-ray. Bitewings show details of the upper and lower teeth in one area of the mouth.

[b]A sealant is a thin, clear or white resin substance that is applied to the biting surfaces of teeth to prevent decay.

[c]Sealants are covered only for unrestored permanent molars and children less than 19 years of age.

[d]A space maintainer is an appliance for a child that keeps space open to allow a permanent tooth to erupt and come into place. The mouth has four quadrants and two arches.

[e]Space maintainers are covered for children less than 19 years of age.

[f] Prefabricated crowns are used on permanent teeth primarily as a temporary measure. For children, prefabricated crowns are commonly used on primary, or baby, teeth. Prefabricated crowns in this table are available in stainless steel.

Table 6. Coverage and Coverage Limits for Selected Dental Services in the State Children's Health Insurance Program (CHIP) Plan and Qualified Health Plan (QHP) GAO Reviewed in New York, Calendar Year 2014

		CHIP plan		QHP	
Service		**Covered**	**Limits**	**Covered**	**Limits**
Routine	Periodic oral exam	Y	2 per year	Y	2 per year
	Cleaning	Y	2 per year	Y	2 per year
	X-rays[a]	Y	Complete 1 every 3 years and bitewings 1 every 2 years or panoramic: 1 every 3 years	Y	Complete 1 every 3 years and bitewings 1 every 2 years or panoramic: 1 every 3 years and other x-rays if medically necessary
	Fluoride treatment (gel or foam)	Y	2 per year[b]	Y	2 per year[b]

Service			CHIP plan		QHP
		Covered	Limits	Covered	Limits
	Sealants[c]	Y	None	Y	None
	Space maintainers[d]	Y	None	Y	None
Other	Fillings	Y	None	Y	None
	Crowns	Y	None	Y	None
	Root canals	Y	None	Y	None
	Dentures	Y	None	Y	None

Source: GAO analysis of information from the state and QHP. | GAO-15-323

Note: CHIP plan information was provided by state officials. QHP information is from the Evidence of Coverage for the New York MetroPlus SilverPlus S1 plan and state and QHP officials.

[a]Complete x-rays cover the entire mouth. Panoramic x-rays show the entire mouth area on a single x-ray. Bitewings show details of the upper and lower teeth in one area of the mouth.

[b]Fluoride is available in places where the local water is not fluoridated.

[c]A sealant is a thin, clear or white resin substance that is applied to the biting surfaces of teeth to prevent decay.

[d]A space maintainer is an appliance for a child that keeps space open to allow a permanent tooth to erupt and come into place. The mouth has four quadrants and two arches.

Table 7. Coverage and Coverage Limits for Selected Dental Services in the State Children's Health Insurance Program (CHIP) Plan and Stand-alone Dental Plan (SADP) GAO Reviewed in Utah, Calendar Year 2014

		CHIP plan		High SADP		Low SADP	
Service		Covered	Limits	Covered	Limits	Covered	Limits
Routine	Periodic oral exam	Y	None	Y	2 per year	Y	2 per year
	Cleaning	Y	2 per year	Y	2 per year	Y	2 per year
	X-raysa	Y	None	Y	• Complete or panoramic: 1 every 3 years • Bitewings: 2 per year	Y	• Complete or panoramic: 1 every 3 years • Bitewings: 2 peryear
	Fluoride treatment (gel or foam)	Y	None	Y	2 per year	Y	2 per year
	Sealantsb	Y	None	Yc	1 every 5 years	Yc	1 every 5 years
	Space maintainersd	Y	None	N	Not covered	N	Not covered
Other	Fillings	Y	None	N	Not covered	N	Not covered
	Crowns	Y	None	N	Not covered	N	Not covered
	Root canals	Y	None	N	Not covered	N	Not covered
	Dentures	Y	None	N	Not covered	N	Not covered

Source: GAO analysis of information from the state and SADP. | GAO-15-323

Notes: CHIP plan information was provided by state officials. SADP information is from Evidences of Coverage for the Utah SelectHealth Dental Fundamental $22 Copay (low SADP) and $10 Copay (high SADP).

SADPs are categorized as "high" and "low" level plans, with 85 and 70 percent actuarial value (AV), respectively. AV indicates the proportion of allowable charges that a health plan will pay, on average—the higher the AV, the lower the cost-sharing expected to be paid by consumers.

[a]Complete x-rays cover the entire mouth. Panoramic x-rays show the entire mouth area on a single x-ray. Bitewings show details of the upper and lower teeth in one area of the mouth.

[b]A sealant is a thin, clear or white resin substance that is applied to the biting surfaces of teeth to prevent decay.

[c]Sealants in the High and Low SADPs are only covered for permanent molars and bicuspids without decay or restoration for children under age 15.

[d]A space maintainer is an appliance for a child that keeps space open to allow a permanent tooth to erupt and come into place. The mouth has four quadrants and two arches.

Table 8. Cost-Sharing Amounts for Selected Dental Services in the State Children's Health Insurance Program (CHIP) Plan and Stand-alone Dental Plan (SADP) GAO Reviewed in Colorado, Calendar Year 2014

		CHIP plan Deductibles and copay/coinsurance by household income as percent of federal poverty level (FPL)				SADP
		143-156%	**157-213%**	**214-260%**	**High**	**Low**
Deductible	Individual	None	None	None	$50	$50
	Family	None	None	None	$150	N/A[a]
Routine Services (copayment=$, coinsurance=%)						
Oral Exam/Evaluation		$0	$0	$0	0% [b]	10% [b]
Cleaning (prophylaxis)		$0	$0	$0	0% [b]	10% [b]
[c](Complete, panoramic, and/or bitewings) X-rays		$0	$0	$0	0% [b]	10% [b]
Fluoride treatment (no varnish)		$0	$0	$0	0% [b]	10% [b]
Sealants[d]		$0	$0	$0	0% [b]	10% [b]
Space maintainers[e]		$0	$0	$0	0% [b]	10% [b]

Table 8. (Continued)

		CHIP plan Deductibles and copay/coinsurance by household income as percent of federal poverty level (FPL)			SADP	
		143-156%	157-213%	214-260%	High	Low
Other Services (copayment=$, coinsurance=%)						
Fillings		$0	$5	$10	40%	50%
Crowns		$0	$5	$10	40%	50%
Root canals (endodontics)		$0	$5	$10	40%	50%
Dentures		$0	$5	$10	40%	Not covered

Source: GAO analysis of information from the state and SADPs. | GAO-15-323

Notes: CHIP plan information was provided by state officials. SADP information is from Evidences of Coverage for the Colorado Anthem Dental Pediatric (low SADP) and Delta Dental Family Plan – Mesa (high SADP) and state officials.

SADPs are categorized as “high” and “low” level plans, with 85 and 70 percent actuarial value (AV), respectively. AV indicates the proportion of allowable charges that a health plan will pay, on average—the higher the AV, the lower the cost-sharing expected to be paid by consumers.

A deductible is a specified amount that must be paid by the consumer before the health plan will begin paying for covered services. A copayment is a fixed dollar amount that a consumer must pay at the time a covered service is provided, such as a $25 payment for a physician visit. Coinsurance is a fixed percentage of the total cost of covered services that a consumer must pay. Health plans may also have an explicit limit on the maximum out-of-pocket costs a consumer could incur.

For the SADPs, the coinsurance amounts (numbers depicted in the table as a percentage) apply once the deductible is met and count toward the out-of-pocket maximum cost. Copayments (numbers depicted in the table with a dollar sign) are paid each time a consumer receives a service, are not subject to the deductible, and do not count toward the out-of-pocket maximum cost.

[a]There was no family option with the selected Low SADP for Colorado. [b]This coinsurance is not subject to the deductible.

[c]Complete x-rays cover the entire mouth. Panoramic x-rays show the entire mouth area on a single x-ray. Bitewings show details of the upper and lower teeth in one area of the mouth.

[d]A sealant is a thin, clear or white resin substance that is applied to the biting surfaces of teeth to prevent decay.

[e]A space maintainer is an appliance for a child that keeps space open to allow a permanent tooth to erupt and come into place.

Table 9. Cost-Sharing Amounts for Selected Dental Services in the State Children's Health Insurance Program (CHIP) Plan and Stand-alone Dental Plan (SADP) GAO Reviewed in Illinois, Calendar Year 2014

		CHIP plan Deductibles and copay/coinsurance by household income as percent of federal poverty level (FPL)			SADP	
		>142-157%	**>157-209%**	**>209-313%**	**High**	**Low**
Deductible	Individual	None	None	None	$25	$45
	Family	None	None	None	N/A	N/A
Routine Services (copayment=$, coinsurance=%)						
Oral Exam/Evaluation		$0	$0	$0	0%[a]	0%
Cleaning (prophylaxis)		$0	$0	$0	0%[a]	0%
X-rays[b] (Complete, panoramic, and/or bitewings)		$0	$0	$0	0%[a]	0%
Fluoride treatment (no varnish)		$0	$0	$0	0%[a]	0%
Sealants[c]		$0	$0	$0	0%[a]	0%
Space maintainers[d]		$0	$0	$0	0%[a]	0%

Table 9. (Continued)

		CHIP plan Deductibles and copay/coinsurance by household income as percent of federal poverty level (FPL)			SADP	
		>142-157%	>157-209%	>209-313%	High	Low
Other Services (copayment=$, coinsurance=%)						
Fillings		$3.90	$5	$10	20%	50%
Crowns[e]		$3.90	$5	$10	20/50%[f]	50%
Root canals (endodontics)		$3.90	$5	$10	50%	50%
Dentures		$3.90	$5	$10	50%	50%

Source: GAO analysis of information from the state and SADP. | GAO-15-323

Notes: CHIP plan information was provided by state officials. SADP information is from Evidences of Coverage for the Illinois Dentegra Dental PPO Children's 70 (low SADP) and 85 (high SADP) plan and state and SADP officials.

SADPs are categorized as "high" and "low" level plans, with 85 and 70 percent actuarial value (AV), respectively. AV indicates the proportion of allowable charges that a health plan will pay, on average—the higher the AV, the lower the cost-sharing expected to be paid by consumers.

A deductible is a specified amount that must be paid by the consumer before the health plan will begin paying for covered services. A copayment is a fixed dollar amount that a consumer must pay at the time a covered service is provided, such as a $25 payment for a physician visit. Coinsurance is a fixed percentage of the total cost of covered services that a consumer must pay. Health plans may also have an explicit limit on the maximum out-of-pocket costs a consumer could incur.

For the SADP, the coinsurance amounts (numbers depicted in the table as a percentage) apply once the deductible is met and count toward the out-of-pocket maximum cost. Copayments (numbers depicted in the table with a dollar sign) are paid each time a consumer receives a service, are not subject to the deductible, and do not count toward the out-of-pocket maximum cost.

[a]This coinsurance is not subject to the deductible.

[b]Complete x-rays cover the entire mouth. Panoramic x-rays show the entire mouth area on a single x-ray. Bitewings show details of the upper and lower teeth in one area of the mouth.

[c]A sealant is a thin, clear or white resin substance that is applied to the biting surfaces of teeth to prevent decay.

[d]A space maintainer is an appliance for a child that keeps space open to allow a permanent tooth to erupt and come into place.

[e]Prefabricated crowns are used on permanent teeth primarily as a temporary measure. For children, prefabricated crowns are commonly used on primary, or baby, teeth

[f] Prefabricated crowns are a basic service and are covered with 20 percent coinsurance to enrollees. Permanent (porcelain, cast, etc) crowns are a major service and covered at 50 percent.

Table 10. Cost-Sharing Amounts for Selected Dental Services in the State Children's Health Insurance Program (CHIP) Plan and Stand-alone Dental Plan (SADP) GAO Reviewed in Kansas, Calendar Year 2014

	CHIP plan			
	Deductibles and copay/coinsurance by household income as percent of federal poverty level (FPL)			**SADP**
		134-242%	**High**	**Low**
Deductible	Individual	None	$50	$50
	Family	None	N/A	N/A
Routine Services (copayment=$, coinsurance=%)				
Oral Exam/Evaluation		$0	0%	0%
Cleaning (prophylaxis)		$0	0%	0%
X-rays[a] (Complete, panoramic, and/or bitewings)	$0		0%	0%
Fluoride treatment (no varnish)	$0		0%	0%
Sealants[b]	$0		0%	0%
Space maintainers[c]	$0		0%	0%

Table 10. (Continued)

	CHIP plan			
	Deductibles and copay/coinsurance by household income as percent of federal poverty level (FPL)			SADP
		134-242%	High	Low
Other Services (copayment=$, coinsurance=%)				
Fillings	$0		20%	40%
Crowns[d]	$0		20/50%[e]	40/50%[f]
Root canals (endodontics)	$0		50%	50%
Dentures	$0		50%	50%

Source: GAO analysis of information from the state and SADP. | GAO-15-323

Notes: CHIP plan information was provided by state officials. SADP information is from Evidences of Coverage for the Kansas Best One Dental Basic- Silver (low SADP) and Best Life Best One Dental Plus- Gold (high SADP).

SADPs are categorized as "high" and "low" level plans, with 85 and 70 percent actuarial value (AV), respectively. AV indicates the proportion of allowable charges that a health plan will pay, on average—the higher the AV, the lower the cost-sharing expected to be paid by consumers.

A deductible is a specified amount that must be paid by the consumer before the health plan will begin paying for covered services. A copayment is a fixed dollar amount that a consumer must pay at the time a covered service is provided, such as a $25 payment for a physician visit. Coinsurance is a fixed percentage of the total cost of covered services that a consumer must pay. Health plans may also have an explicit limit on the maximum out-of-pocket costs a consumer could incur.

For the SADP, the coinsurance amounts (numbers depicted in the table as a percentage) apply once the deductible is met and count toward the out-of-pocket maximum cost. Copayments (numbers depicted in the table with a dollar sign) are paid each time a consumer receives a service, are not subject to the deductible, and do not count toward the out-of-pocket maximum cost.

[a]Complete x-rays cover the entire mouth. Panoramic x-rays show the entire mouth area on a single x-ray. Bitewings show details of the upper and lower teeth in one area of the mouth.

[b]A sealant is a thin, clear, or white resin substance that is applied to the biting surfaces of teeth to prevent decay.

[c]A space maintainer is an appliance for a child that keeps space open to allow a permanent tooth to erupt and come into place.

[d]Prefabricated crowns are used on permanent teeth primarily as a temporary measure. For children, prefabricated crowns are commonly used on primary, or baby, teeth.

[e]Prefabricated crowns are a basic service and are covered with 20 percent coinsurance to enrollees. Permanent (porcelain, cast, etc.) crowns are a major service and covered at 50 percent.

[f] Prefabricated crowns are a basic service and are covered with 40 percent coinsurance to enrollees. Permanent (porcelain, cast, etc.) crowns are a major service and covered at 50 percent.

Table 11. Cost-Sharing Amounts for Selected Dental Services in the State Children's Health Insurance Program (CHIP) Plan and Qualified Health Plan (QHP) GAO Reviewed in New York, Calendar Year 2014

		Deductibles and copay/coinsurance by household income as percent of federal poverty level (FPL)				
		CHIP plan		QHP		
		>154-400%	100-150%	>150-200%	>200-250%	>250-400%
Deductible	Individual	None	$0	$250	$1,750	$2,000
	Family	None	$0	$500	$3,500	$4,000
Routine Services (copayment=$, coinsurance=%)						
Oral Exam/Evaluation		$0	$10	$15	$30	$35
Cleaning (prophylaxis)		$0	$10	$15	$30	$35
X-rays[a] (Complete, panoramic, and/or bitewings)		$0	$10	$15	$30	$35
Fluoride treatment (no varnish)		$0	$10	$15	$30	$35
Sealants[b]		$0	$10	$15	$30	$35
Space maintainers[c]		$0	$10	$15	$30	$35

Table 11. (Continued)

		Deductibles and copay/coinsurance by household income as percent of federal poverty level (FPL)				
		CHIP plan		**QHP**		
		>154-400%	**100-150%**	**>150-200%**	**>200-250%**	**>250-400%**
Other Services (copayment=$, coinsurance=%)						
Fillings		$0	$10	$15	$30	$35
Crowns		$0	$10	$15	$30	$35
Root canals (endodontics)		$0	$10	$15	$30	$35
Dentures		$0	$10	$15	$30	$35

Source: GAO analysis of information from the state and QHP. | GAO-15-323

Notes: CHIP plan information was provided by state officials. QHP information is from Evidences of Coverage for the New York MetroPlus SilverPlus S1 plan and state and QHP officials.

For the QHP in this table, the FPL ranges correspond with the following actuarial value (AV) levels: 100-150 percent FPL (94 percent AV), >150-200 percent FPL (87 percent AV), >200-250 percent FPL (73 percent AV), and >250-400 percent FPL (70 percent AV).

A deductible is a specified amount that must be paid by the consumer before the health plan will begin paying for covered services. A copayment is a fixed dollar amount that a consumer must pay at the time a covered service is provided, such as a $25 payment for a physician visit. Coinsurance is a fixed percentage of the total cost of covered services that a consumer must pay. Health plans may also have an explicit limit on the maximum out-of-pocket costs a consumer could incur.

For the QHP, the coinsurance amounts (numbers depicted in the table as a percentage) apply once the deductible is met and count toward the out-of-pocket maximum cost. Copayments (numbers depicted in the table with a dollar sign) are paid each time a consumer receives a service, are not subject to the deductible, and count toward the out-of-pocket maximum cost.

[a] Complete x-rays cover the entire mouth. Panoramic x-rays show the entire mouth area on a single x-ray. Bitewings show details of the upper and lower teeth in one area of the mouth.

[b] A sealant is a thin, clear, or white resin substance that is applied to the biting surfaces of teeth to prevent decay.

[c] A space maintainer is an appliance for a child that keeps space open to allow a permanent tooth to erupt and come into place.

Table 12. Cost-Sharing Amounts for Selected Dental Services in the State Children's Health Insurance Program (CHIP) Plan and Stand-alone Dental Plan (SADP) GAO Reviewed in Utah, Calendar Year 2014

		CHIP plan Deductibles and copay/coinsurance by household income as percent of federal poverty level (FPL)		SADP	
		134-150%	**151-200%**	**High**	**Low**
Deductible	Individual	None	$50	$0	$0
	Family	None	$150	N/A	N/A
Routine Services (copayment= $, coinsurance=%)					
Oral Exam/Evaluation		$0	$0	$10	$22
Cleaning (prophylaxis)		$0	$0	$10	$22
X-rays[a] (Complete, panoramic, and/or bitewings)		$0	$0	$10	$22
Fluoride treatment (no varnish)		$0	$0	$10	$22
Sealants[b]		$0	$0	$10	$22
Space maintainers[c]		$0	$0	Not covered	Not covered
Other Services (copayment=$, coinsurance=%)					
Fillings		5% [d]	20%	Not covered	Not covered
Crowns		5% [d]	20%	Not covered	Not covered
Root canals (endodontics)		5% [d]	20%	Not covered	Not covered
Dentures		5% [d]	20%	Not covered	Not covered

Source: GAO analysis of information from the state and SADP. | GAO-15-323

Notes: CHIP plan information was provided by state officials. SADP information is from Evidences of Coverage for the Utah SelectHealth Dental Fundamental $22 Copay (low SADP) and $10 Copay (high SADP).

SADPs are categorized as “high” and “low” level plans, with 85 and 70 percent actuarial value (AV), respectively. AV indicates the proportion of allowable charges that a health plan will pay, on average—the higher the AV, the lower the cost-sharing expected to be paid by consumers.

A deductible is a specified amount that must be paid by the consumer before the health plan will begin paying for covered services. A copayment is a fixed dollar amount that a consumer must pay at the time a covered service is provided, such as a $25 payment for a physician visit. Coinsurance is a fixed percentage of the total cost of covered services that a consumer must pay. Health plans may also have an explicit limit on the maximum out-of-pocket costs a consumer could incur.

For the SADP, the coinsurance amounts (numbers depicted in the table as a percentage) apply once the deductible is met and count toward the out-of-pocket maximum cost. Copayments (numbers depicted in the table with a dollar sign) are paid each time a consumer receives a service, are not subject to the deductible, and count toward the out-of-pocket maximum cost.

Plan officials indicated that the SADP reviewed would be discontinued effective 12/31/2014, as the dental benefits offered would be embedded in SelectHealth’s medical plans in 2015.

[a]Complete x-rays cover the entire mouth. Panoramic x-rays show the entire mouth area on a single x-ray. Bitewings show details of the upper and lower teeth in one area of the mouth.

[b]A sealant is a thin, clear, or white resin substance that is applied to the biting surfaces of teeth to prevent decay.

[c]A space maintainer is an appliance for a child that keeps space open to allow a permanent tooth to erupt and come into place.

[d]This coinsurance is not subject to the deductible.

APPENDIX IV: COST-SHARING FOR SELECTED SERVICES IN CHIP PLANS AND QHPS GAO REVIEWED IN FIVE STATES

Tables 13 through 17 provide information on cost-sharing—deductibles, copayments, and coinsurance—for selected services in State Children's Health Insurance Program (CHIP) plans and qualified health plans (QHP) we reviewed in five states: Colorado, Illinois, Kansas, New York, and Utah. For selected CHIP plans and QHPs, we note differences in cost-sharing amounts by income level.

For selected QHPs, these variations reflect the cost-sharing subsidies that are available to certain enrollees.[1] For all five states, cost-sharing amounts were subject to out-of-pocket maximum costs. For CHIP enrollees in each state, cost-sharing and premium amounts were subject to a federally established out-of-pocket maximum cost equal to 5 percent of a family's income.

For QHP enrollees, issuers established an out-of-pocket maximum cost for each plan that was equal to or less than out-of-pocket maximum costs established under the Patient Protection and Affordable Care Act (PPACA).

PPACA out-of-pocket maximum costs for households with incomes between 100 and 400 percent of the federal poverty level (FPL) in 2014 ranged from $2,250 to $6,350 for individuals and $4,500 to $12,700 for families.

These out-of-pocket maximum costs do not include costs associated with services provided through a SADP and, in contrast to CHIP, these out-of-pocket maximum costs do not include premiums.

Table 13. Cost-Sharing Amounts for Selected Services in the State Children's Health Insurance Program (CHIP) Plan and Qualified Health Plan (QHP) GAO Reviewed in Colorado, Calendar Year 2014

		Deductibles and copay/coinsurance by household income as percent of federal poverty level (FPL)						
		CHIP plan			QHP			
		143-156%	157-213%	214-260%	100-150%	>150-200%	>200-250%	>250-400%
Plan deductible	Individual	None	None	None	$500	$900	$3,250	$4,600
	Family	None	None	None	$1,000	$1,800	$6,500	$9,200
Prescription drug deductible	Individual	None	None	None	$250	$500	$1,000	$1,500
	Family	None	None	None	$500	$1,000	$2,000	$3,000
Service (copayment=$, coinsurance=%)								
Ambulatory patient services: office visits	Primary care physician	$2	$5	$10	$25	$25	$25	$25
	Specialty physician	$2	$5	$10	$35	$35	$35	$35
Emergency care		$3	$30	$50	20%	20%	20%	20%
Inpatient hospital		$2	$20	$50	20%	20%	20%	20%
Maternity care		$0	$0	$0	20%	20%	20%	20%
Mental health and substance abuse	Inpatient	$2	$20	$50	20%	20%	20%	20%
	Outpatient	$2	$5	$10	20%	20%	20%	20%
Prescription drugs	Generic	$1	$3	$5	$10[a]	$10[a]	$10[a]	$10[a]
	Brand-name	$1	$10	$15	$50[b]	$50[b]	$50[b]	$50[b]

		Deductibles and copay/coinsurance by household income as percent of federal poverty level (FPL)						
		CHIP plan			QHP			
		143-156%	157-213%	214-260%	100-150%	>150-200%	>200-250%	>250-400%
Outpatient therapies (occupational, physical, speech)	Rehabilitative	$2	$5	$10	20%	20%	20%	20%
	Habilitative	$2	$5	$10	20%	20%	20%	20%
Preventive care		$0	$0	$0	0%[c]	0%[c]	0%[c]	0%[c]
Pediatric vision	Optometrist exam	$0	$0	$0	0%[c]	0%[c]	0%[c]	0%[c]
	Corrective lenses	$0	$0	$0	50%	50%	50%	50%
Pediatric hearing	Testing	$0	$0	$0	0%[c]	0%[c]	0%[c]	0%[c]
	Hearing aids	$0	$0	$0	20%	20%	20%	20%
Durable medical equipment		$0	$0	$0	20%	20%	20%	20%
Home- and community-based health care		$0	$0	$0	20%	20%	20%	20%
Enabling Services	Non-hospice respite care	Not covered	Not covered	Not covered	Not covered	Not covered	Not covered	Notcovered
	Translation services—office visits	$0	$0	$0	Not covered	Not covered	Not covered	Notcovered
	Care coordination/ case management	$0	$0	$0	Not covered	Not covered	Not covered	Notcovered
	Routine transportation[d]	Not covered	Not covered	Not covered	Not covered	Not covered	Not covered	Notcovered

Source: GAO analysis of information from the state and QHP. | GAO-15-323

Notes: CHIP plan information is from state officials. QHP information is from Evidences of Coverage for the Colorado Humana Connect Silver 4600/6300 Plan and state and QHP officials.

For the QHP in this table, the FPL ranges correspond with the following actuarial value (AV) levels: 100-150 percent FPL (94 percent AV), >150-200 percent FPL (87 percent AV), >200-250 percent FPL (73 percent AV), and >250-400 percent FPL (70 percent AV).

A deductible is a specified amount that must be paid by the consumer before the health plan will begin paying for covered services. A copayment is a fixed dollar amount that a consumer must pay at the time a covered service is provided, such as a $25 payment for a physician visit. Coinsurance is a fixed percentage of the total cost of covered services that a consumer must pay. Health plans may also have an explicit limit on the maximum out-of-pocket costs a consumer could incur.

For the QHP, the coinsurance amounts (numbers depicted in the table as a percentage) apply once the deductible is met and count toward the out-of-pocket maximum cost. Copayments (numbers depicted in the table with a dollar sign) are paid each time a consumer receives a service, are not subject to the deductible, and do not count toward the out-of-pocket maximum cost.

Rehabilitation is provided to help a person regain, maintain or prevent deterioration of a skill that has been acquired but then lost or impaired due to illness, injury, or disabling condition. While federal law does not define habilitative services, habilitation has been defined by several advocacy groups as a service that is provided in order for a person to attain, maintain, or prevent deterioration of a skill or function never learned or acquired due to a disabling condition.

The Patient Protection and Affordable Care Act (PPACA) required that, effective January 1, 2014, states determine Medicaid and CHIP income eligibility for certain categories of individuals using a uniform modified adjusted gross income (MAGI) methodology that is derived from a federal tax based definition of income. To accomplish this, states were required to convert their net income eligibility standards to MAGI equivalent income standards. The CHIP eligibility FPL ranges in this table reflect this conversion. Additionally, PPACA specifies that an income disregard equal to five percentage points of the FPL be deducted from an individual's income when determining Medicaid and CHIP eligibility. The FPL eligibility ranges in this table do not reflect this income disregard.

[a]If generic prescription drugs are ordered through the mail, the cost per prescription is $20 for a 90-day supply and is subject to the prescription deductible.

[b]Brand-name prescription drugs are subject to the prescription deductible. If brand-name prescription drugs are ordered through the mail, the cost per prescription is $100 for a 90-day supply and is subject to the prescription deductible. Brand- name drugs include drugs designated by the plan as "preferred" or included in their formulary.

[c]This coinsurance is not subject to the deductible.

[d]Routine transportation includes transportation to and from medical appointments.

Table 14. Cost-Sharing Amounts for Selected Services in the State Children's Health Insurance Program (CHIP) Plan and Qualified Health Plan (QHP) GAO Reviewed in Illinois, Calendar Year 2014

		Deductibles and copay/coinsurance by household income as percent of federal poverty level (FPL)						
		CHIP plan					QHP	
		>142-157%	>157-209%	>209-313%	100-150%	>150-200%	>200-250%	>250-400%
Plan deductible	Individual	None	None	None	$500	$1,500	$5,000	$6,000
	Family	None	None	None	$1,500	$4,500	$10,400	$12,700
Service (copayment=$, coinsurance=%)								
Ambulatory patient services: office visits	Primary care physician	$3.90	$5	$10	$30	$30	$30	$30
	Specialty physician	$3.90	$5	$10	$50	$50	$50	$50
Emergency care		$0	$5	$30	0%	0%	0%	0%
Inpatient hospital		$3.90a	$5a	$100	0%	0%	0%	0%
Maternity care		$0	$0	$0	0%	0%	0%	0%
Mental health and substance abuse	Inpatient	$0	$0	$0	0%	0%	0%	0%
	Outpatient therapy	$3.90b	$5b	$10b	0%	0%	0%	0%
Prescription drugs	Generic	$2	$3	$3	$0c	$0c	$0c	$0c
	Brand-name	$3.90	$5	$7	$50d	$50d	$50d	$50d
Outpatient therapies (occupational, physical, speech)	Rehabilitative	$0	$0	$0	0%	0%	0%	0%

Table 14. (Continued)

		Deductibles and copay/coinsurance by household income as percent of federal poverty level (FPL)						
		CHIP plan					**QHP**	
		>142-157%	**>157-209%**	**>209-313%**	**100-150%**	**>150-200%**	**>200-250%**	**>250-400%**
	Habilitative	$0	$0	$0	0%	0%	0%	0%
Preventive care		$0	$0	$0	0%e	0%e	0%e	0%e
Pediatric vision	Optometrist exam	$3.90	$5	$10	$0	$0	$0	$0
	Corrective lenses	$0	$0	$0	0%	0%	0%	0%
Pediatric hearing	Testing	$0	$0	$0	$30	$30	$30	$30
	Hearing aids	$0	$0	$0	0%	0%	0%	0%
Durable medical equipment		$0	$0	$0	0%	0%	0%	0%
Home- and community-based health care		$0	$0	$0	0%	0%	0%	0%
Hospice		$0	$0	$0	$250f	$250f	$250f	$250f
Enabling services								
	Non-hospice respite care	Not covered	Not covered	Not covered	Not covered	Not covered	Not covered	Notcovered
	Translation services—office visits	Not covered	Not covered	Not covered	Not covered	Not covered	Not covered	Notcovered

		Deductibles and copay/coinsurance by household income as percent of federal poverty level (FPL)						
		CHIP plan					**QHP**	
		>142-157%	**>157-209%**	**>209-313%**	**100-150%**	**>150-200%**	**>200-250%**	**>250-400%**
	Care coordination/ case management	Not covered	Not covered	Not covered	0%	0%	0%	0%
	Routine transportationg	$0	$0	Not covered	Not covered	Not covered	Not covered	Notcovered

Source: GAO analysis of information from the state and QHP. | GAO-15-323

Notes: CHIP plan information is from state officials. QHP information is from Evidences of Coverage for the Illinois Blue Choice Silver PPO 003 Plan and state and QHP officials.

For the QHP in this table, the FPL ranges correspond with the following actuarial value (AV) levels: 100-150 percent FPL (94 percent AV), >150-200 percent FPL (87 percent AV), >200-250 percent FPL (73 percent AV), and >250-400 percent FPL (70 percent AV).

A deductible is a specified amount that must be paid by the consumer before the health plan will begin paying for covered services. A copayment is a fixed dollar amount that a consumer must pay at the time a covered service is provided, such as a $25 payment for a physician visit. Coinsurance is a fixed percentage of the total cost of covered services that a consumer must pay. Health plans may also have an explicit limit on the maximum out-of-pocket costs a consumer could incur.

For the QHP, the coinsurance amounts (numbers depicted in the table as a percentage) apply once the deductible is met and count toward the out-of-pocket maximum cost. Copayments (numbers depicted in the table with a dollar sign) are paid each time a consumer receives a service, are not subject to the deductible, and count toward the out-of-pocket maximum cost.

Rehabilitation is provided to help a person regain, maintain or prevent deterioration of a skill that has been acquired but then lost or impaired due to illness, injury, or disabling condition. While federal law does not define habilitative services, habilitation has been defined by several advocacy groups as a service that is provided in order for a person to attain, maintain, or prevent deterioration of a skill or function never learned or acquired due to a disabling condition.

The Patient Protection and Affordable Care Act (PPACA) required that, effective January 1, 2014, states determine Medicaid and CHIP income eligibility for certain categories of individuals using a uniform modified adjusted gross income (MAGI) methodology that is derived from a federal tax based definition of income. To accomplish this, states were required to convert their net income eligibility standards to MAGI equivalent income standards. The CHIP eligibility FPL ranges in this table reflect this conversion. Additionally, PPACA specifies that an income disregard equal to five percentage points of the FPL be deducted from an individual's income when determining Medicaid and CHIP eligibility. The FPL eligibility ranges in this table do not reflect this income disregard.

[a]The copayment amount is charged per day.

[b]Listed copayment is charged when mental health and substance abuse outpatient therapy is provided in a Federally Qualified Health Center or Rural Health Center.

[c]If generic prescription drugs are ordered through the mail, the cost per prescription is $0.

[d]If brand-name prescription drugs are ordered through the mail, the cost per prescription is $100. Brand- name drugs include drugs designated by the plan as "preferred" or included in their formulary.

[e]This coinsurance is not subject to the deductible.

[f]Hospice care has a $250 per admission deductible. For inpatient covered services, 100 percent of the eligible charge is covered.

[g]Routine transportation includes transportation to and from medical appointments.

Table 15. Cost-Sharing Amounts for Selected Services in the State Children's Health Insurance Program (CHIP) Plan and Qualified Health Plan (QHP) GAO Reviewed in Kansas, Calendar Year 2014

		Deductibles and copay/coinsurance by household income as percent of federal poverty level (FPL)				
		CHIP plan		QHP		
		134-242%	100-150%	>150-200%	>200-250%	>250-400%
Plan deductible	Individual	None	$0	$0	$2,000	$2,000
	Family	None	$0	$0	$4,000	$4,000
Prescription drug deductible	Individual	None	None	None	$2,000	$2,000

		Deductibles and copay/coinsurance by household income as percent of federal poverty level (FPL)				
		CHIP plan		QHP		
		134-242%	100-150%	>150-200%	>200-250%	>250-400%
Service (copayment=$, coinsurance=%)						
Ambulatory patient services: office visits	Primary care physician	$0	$0	$5	$5	$10
	Specialty physician	$0	$20	$40	$75[a]	$75[a]
Emergency care		$0	$100	$250	$500[b]	$500[b]
Inpatient hospital		$0	10%	30%	30%	50%
Maternity care		$0	Various [c]	Various [d]	Various[d]	Various[e]
Mental health and substance abuse	Inpatient	$0	10%	30%	30%	50%
	Outpatient therapy	$0	10%	30%	30%	50%
Prescription drugs	Generic	$0	$5[f]	$10[f]	$15[f]	$10 [f]
	Brand-name	$0	$30 [g]	$35 [g]	$45 [g,h]	$45 [g,h]
Outpatient therapies (occupational, physical, speech)	Rehabilitative	$0	10%	30%	30%	50%
	Habilitative	Not covered	10%	30%	30%	50%
Preventive care		$0	$0	$0	$0	$0
Pediatric vision	Optometrist exam	$0	$0	$0	$0	$0
	Corrective lenses	$0	$0	$0	$0	$0
Pediatric hearing	Testing (screening or exam)	$0	0% i	0%[i]	0%[i]	0%[i]
	Hearing aids	$0	10%	30%	30%	50%
Durable medical equipment		$0	10%	30%	30%	50%
Home and community-based health care		$0	10%	30%	30%	50%
Hospice		$0	10%	30%	30%	50%

Table 15. (Continued)

		Deductibles and copay/coinsurance by household income as percent of federal poverty level (FPL)				
		CHIP plan		QHP		
		134-242%	100-150%	>150-200%	>200-250%	>250-400%
Enabling services	Non-hospice respite care	$0	Not covered	Not covered	Not covered	Not covered
	Translation services—office visits	$0	Not covered	Not covered	Not covered	Not covered
	Care coordination/ case management	$0	Not covered	Not covered	Not covered	Not covered
	Routine transportation[j]	$0	Not covered	Not covered	Not covered	Not covered

Source: GAO analysis of information from the state and QHP. | GAO-15-323

Notes: CHIP plan information is from state officials. QHP information is from Evidences of Coverage for the Kansas Coventry Health and Life Integrated Silver $10 Copay PPO KC Exchange Plan and state and QHP officials.

For the QHP in this table, the FPL ranges correspond with the following actuarial value (AV) levels: 100-150 percent FPL (94 percent AV), >150-200 percent FPL (87 percent AV), >200-250 percent FPL (73 percent AV), and >250-400 percent FPL (70 percent AV).

A deductible is a specified amount that must be paid by the consumer before the health plan will begin paying for covered services. A copayment is a fixed dollar amount that a consumer must pay at the time a covered service is provided, such as a $25 payment for a physician visit. Coinsurance is a fixed percentage of the total cost of covered services that a consumer must pay. Health plans may also have an explicit limit on the maximum out-of-pocket costs a consumer could incur.

For the QHP, the coinsurance amounts (numbers depicted in the table as a percentage) apply once the deductible is met and count toward the out-of-pocket maximum cost. Copayments (numbers depicted in the table with a dollar sign) are paid each time a consumer receives a service, are not subject to the deductible, and count toward the out-of-pocket maximum cost.

Rehabilitation is provided to help a person regain, maintain or prevent deterioration of a skill that has been acquired but then lost or impaired due to illness, injury, or disabling condition. While federal law does not define habilitative services, habilitation has been defined by several advocacy groups as a service that is provided in order for a person to attain, maintain, or prevent deterioration of a skill or function never learned or acquired due to a disabling condition.

The Patient Protection and Affordable Care Act (PPACA) required that, effective January 1, 2014, states determine Medicaid and CHIP income eligibility for certain categories of individuals using a uniform modified adjusted gross income (MAGI) methodology that is derived from a federal tax based definition of income. To accomplish this, states were required to convert their net income eligibility standards to MAGI equivalent income standards. The CHIP eligibility FPL ranges in this table reflect this conversion. Additionally, PPACA specifies that an income disregard equal to five percentage points of the FPL be deducted from an individual's income when determining Medicaid and CHIP eligibility. The FPL eligibility ranges in this table do not reflect this income disregard.

[a]The first two specialist visits are charged at $75 and are not subject to the deductible. Three visits or more are charged at $75 and are subject to the deductible.

[b]The first emergency visit is charged at $500 and is not subject to the deductible. Two visits or more are charged at $500 and are subject to the deductible.

[c]Costs for maternity services varied. Prenatal office visits are charged at $0; physician charges, prenatal, postnatal, ultrasound, and delivery are charged a one-time $250; and outpatient ultrasounds are charged at 10 percent.

[d]Costs for maternity services varied. Prenatal office visits are charged at $0; physician charges, prenatal, postnatal, ultrasound, and delivery are charged a one-time $250; and outpatient ultrasounds are charged at 30 percent.

[e]Costs for maternity services varied. Prenatal office visits are charged at $0; physician charges, prenatal, postnatal, ultrasound, and delivery are charged a one-time $250; and outpatient ultrasounds are charged at 50 percent.

[f]The prices displayed are Preferred Generic (Tier 1) prescription drugs. The Kansas QHP also has Best Value Generics (Tier 1A), which is a select list of tier one drugs determined by Coventry to be available for a reduced copayment. Alavert OTC and Chlorpropamide are examples of drugs on this tier. Tier 1A drugs are charged at $3 for the 100-150 percent plan variation and $5 for the >150-200 percent, >200-250 percent and >250-400 percent plan variations.

[g]If brand-name prescription drugs are ordered through the mail, the cost per prescription is $75, $87.50, $112.50 (subject to the prescription deductible) and $112.50 (subject to the prescription deductible) for 100-150 percent, >150-200 percent, >200-250

percent, and >250-400 percent FPL, respectively. Brand-name drugs include drugs designated by the plan as "preferred" or included in their formulary.

[h]Brand-name prescription drugs in the >200-250 percent and >250-400 percent FPL ranges are subject to the prescription deductible.

[i]The prices displayed are not subject to the deductible and apply for preventive hearing testing only. If the service is not billed as preventive, hearing testing would be charged at 10%, 30%, 30% and 50% for 100-150 percent, >150-200 percent, >200-250 percent and >250-400 percent FPL, respectively.

[j] Routine transportation includes transportation to and from medical appointments.

Table 16. Cost-Sharing Amounts for Selected Services in the State Children's Health Insurance Program (CHIP) Plan and Qualified Health Plan (QHP) GAO Reviewed in New York, Calendar Year 2014

		Deductibles and copay/coinsurance by household income as percent of federal poverty level (FPL)				
		CHIP plan			**QHP**	
		>154-400%	**100-150%**	**>150-200%**	**>200-250%**	**>250-400%**
Plan deductible	Individual	None	$0	$250	$1,750	$2,000
	Family	None	$0	$500	$3,500	$4,000
Service (copayment=$, coinsurance=%)						
Ambulatory patient services: office visits	Primary care physician	$0	$10	$15	$30	$30
	Specialty physician	$0	$20	$35	$50	$50
Emergency care		$0	$50[a]	$75[a]	$150[a]	$150[a]
Inpatient hospital		$0	$100	$250	$1,500	$1,500
Maternity care		$0	Various[b]	Various[c]	Various[d]	Various[d]
Mental health and substance abuse	Inpatient	$0	$100	$250	$1,500	$1,500

		Deductibles and copay/coinsurance by household income as percent of federal poverty level (FPL)				
		CHIP plan			**QHP**	
		>154-400%	**100-150%**	**>150-200%**	**>200-250%**	**>250-400%**
	Outpatient therapy	$0	$10	$15	$30	$30
Prescription drugs	Generic	$0	$6[e]	$9[e]	$10[e]	$10[e]
	Brand-name	$0	$15[f]	$20[f]	$35[f]	$35[f]
Outpatient therapies (occupational, physical, speech)	Rehabilitative	$0	$15	$25	$30	$30
	Habilitative	$0	$15	$25	$30	$30
Preventive care		$0	$0	$0	$0	$0
Pediatric vision	Optometrist exam	$0	$10	$15	$30	$35
	Corrective lenses	$0	5%	10%	25%	30%
Pediatric hearing	Testing (screening or exam)	$0	$0	$0	$0	$0
	Hearing aids	$0	5%	10%	25%	30%
Durable medical equipment		$0	5%	10%	25%	30%
Home- and community-based health care		$0	$10	$15	$30	$30
Hospice		$0	$100[g]	$250[g]	$1,500[g]	$1,500[g]
Enabling services	Non-hospice respite care	Not covered	Not covered	Not covered	Not covered	Not covered
	Translation services—office visits	$0	Not covered	Not covered	Not covered	Not covered

Table 16. (Continued)

		Deductibles and copay/coinsurance by household income as percent of federal poverty level (FPL)				
		CHIP plan			**QHP**	
		>154-400%	**100-150%**	**>150-200%**	**>200-250%**	**>250-400%**
	Care coordination/ case management	$0	Not covered	Not covered	Not covered	Not covered
	Routine transportation[h]	Not covered	Not covered	Not covered	Not covered	Not covered

Source: GAO analysis of information from the state and QHP. | GAO-15-323

Notes: CHIP information is from state officials. QHP information is from Evidences of Coverage for the New York MetroPlus SilverPlus S1 Plan and state and QHP officials.

For the QHP in this table, the FPL ranges correspond with the following actuarial value (AV) levels: 100-150 percent FPL (94 percent AV), >150-200 percent FPL (87 percent AV), >200-250 percent FPL (73 percent AV), and >250-400 percent FPL (70 percent AV).

A deductible is a specified amount that must be paid by the consumer before the health plan will begin paying for covered services. A copayment is a fixed dollar amount that a consumer must pay at the time a covered service is provided, such as a $25 payment for a physician visit. Coinsurance is a fixed percentage of the total cost of covered services that a consumer must pay. Health plans may also have an explicit limit on the maximum out-of-pocket costs a consumer could incur.

For the QHP, the coinsurance amounts (numbers depicted in the table as a percentage) apply once the deductible is met and count toward the out-of-pocket maximum cost. Copayments (numbers depicted in the table with a dollar sign) are paid each time a consumer receives a service, are not subject to the deductible, and count toward the out-of-pocket maximum cost.

Rehabilitation is provided to help a person regain, maintain or prevent deterioration of a skill that has been acquired but then lost or impaired due to illness, injury, or disabling condition. While federal law does not define habilitative services, habilitation has been defined by several advocacy groups as a service that is provided in order for a person to attain, maintain, or prevent deterioration of a skill or function never learned or acquired due to a disabling condition.

The Patient Protection and Affordable Care Act (PPACA) required that, effective January 1, 2014, states determine Medicaid and CHIP income eligibility for certain categories of individuals using a uniform modified adjusted gross income (MAGI) methodology that is derived from a federal tax based definition of income. To accomplish this, states were required to convert their net income eligibility standards to MAGI equivalent income standards. The CHIP eligibility FPL ranges in this table reflect this conversion. Additionally, PPACA specifies that an income disregard equal to five percentage points of the FPL be deducted from an individual's income when determining Medicaid and CHIP eligibility. The FPL eligibility ranges in this table do not reflect this income disregard.

[a]Copayment is waived if the patient is admitted as an inpatient directly from the emergency room.

[b]Costs for maternity services varied. Prenatal care is charged at $0, inpatient hospital services are charged at $100, physician and nurse midwife services for delivery are charged at $25, and a breast pump is charged at $0.

[c]Costs for maternity services varied. Prenatal care is charged at $0, inpatient hospital services are charged at $250, physician and nurse midwife services for delivery are charged at $75, and a breast pump is charged at $0.

[d]Costs for maternity services varied. Prenatal care is charged at $0, inpatient hospital services are charged at $1,500, physician and nurse midwife services for delivery are charged at $100, and a breast pump is charged at $0.

[e]If generic prescription drugs are ordered through the mail, the cost per prescription is $15, $23, $25 and $25 for 100-150 percent, >150-200 percent, >200-250 percent and >250-400 percent FPL, respectively, for a 90-day supply.

[f]If brand-name prescription drugs are ordered through the mail, the cost per prescription is $38, $50, $88 and $88 for 100-150 percent, >150-200 percent, >200-250 percent and >250-400 percent FPL, respectively, for a 90-day supply.

[g]QHP cost-sharing displayed is for inpatient hospice. Outpatient hospice is charged at $10, $15, $30 and $30 for 100-150 percent, >150-200 percent, >200-250 percent and >250-400 percent FPL, respectively.

[h]Routine transportation includes transportation to and from medical appointments.

Table 17. Cost-Sharing Amounts for Selected Services in the State Children's Health Insurance Program (CHIP) Plan and Qualified Health Plan (QHP) GAO Reviewed in Utah, Calendar Year 2014

		Deductibles and copay/coinsurance by household income as percent of federal poverty level (FPL)					
		CHIP plan		QHP			
		134-150%	151-200%	100-150%	>150-200%	>200-250%	>250-400%
Plan deductible	Individual	$40	$500	$500	$900	$3,250	$4,600
	Family	$40	$1,500	$1,000	$1,800	$6,500	$9,200
Prescription drug deductible	Individual	$0	$0	$250	$500	$1,000	$1,500
	Family	$0	$0	$500	$1,000	$2,000	$3,000
Service (copayment=$, coinsurance=%)							
Ambulatory patient services: office visits	Primary care physician	$5	$25	$25	$25	$25	$25
	Specialty physician	$5	$40	$35	$35	$35	$35
Emergency care		$5	$300[a]	20%	20%	20%	20%
Inpatient hospital		$150[a]	20%	20%	20%	20%	20%
Maternity care		20%	20%	20%	20%	20%	20%
Mental health	Inpatient	$150[a]	20%	20%	20%	20%	20%
	Outpatient therapy	$5	$0	20%	20%	20%	20%

		Deductibles and copay/coinsurance by household income as percent of federal poverty level (FPL)					
		CHIP plan		**QHP**			
		134-150%	**151-200%**	**100-150%**	**>150-200%**	**>200-250%**	**>250-400%**
Substance abuse	Inpatient	20%	20%	20%	20%	20%	20%
	Outpatient therapy	20%	0%	20%	20%	20%	20%
Prescription drugs	Generic	$5	$15	$10[b]	$10[b]	$10[b]	$10[b]
	Brand-name	5%[d]	25%[d]	$20[c]	$20[c]	$20[c]	$20[c]
Outpatient therapies (occupational, physical, speech)	Rehabilitative	$5	$40[a]	20%	20%	20%	20%
	Habilitative	Not covered	Not covered	20%	20%	20%	20%
Preventive care		$0	$0	0%[d]	0%[d]	0%[d]	0%[d]
Pediatric vision	Optometrist exam	$5	$25	0%[d]	0%[d]	0%[d]	0%[d]
	Corrective lenses	Not covered	Not covered	Not covered	Not covered	Not covered	Not covered
Pediatric hearing	Testing	$5	$25	0%[d]	0%[d]	0%[d]	0%[d]
	Hearing aids	Not covered[e]	Not covered[e]	Not covered	Not covered	Not covered	Not covered
Durable medical equipment		5%	20%	20%	20%	20%	20%
Home- and community-based health care		5%	20%	20%	20%	20%	20%

Table 17. (Continued)

		Deductibles and copay/coinsurance by household income as percent of federal poverty level (FPL)					
		CHIP plan		**QHP**			
		134-150%	**151-200%**	**100-150%**	**>150-200%**	**>200-250%**	**>250-400%**
Hospice		5%	20%	20%	20%	20%	20%
Enabling services	Non-hospice respite care	Not covered	Not covered	Not covered	Not covered	Not covered	Not covered
	Translation services—office visits	$0	$0	Not covered	Not covered	Not covered	Not covered
	Care coordination/case management	$0	$0	Not covered	Not covered	Not covered	Not covered
	Routine transportation[f]	Not covered	Not covered	Not covered	Not covered	Not covered	Not covered

Source: GAO analysis of information from the state and QHP. | GAO-15-323

Notes: CHIP plan information was provided by state officials. QHP information is from Evidences of Coverage for the Utah Humana Connect Silver 4600/6300 Plan and state and QHP officials.

For the QHP in this table, the FPL ranges correspond with the following actuarial value (AV) levels: 100-150 percent FPL (94 percent AV), >150-200 percent FPL (87 percent AV), >200-250 percent FPL (73 percent AV), and >250-400 percent FPL (70 percent AV).

A deductible is a specified amount that must be paid by the consumer before the health plan will begin paying for covered services. A copayment is a fixed dollar amount that a consumer must pay at the time a covered service is provided, such as a $25 payment for a physician visit. Coinsurance is a fixed percentage of the total cost of covered services that a consumer must pay. Health plans may also have an explicit limit on the maximum out-of-pocket costs a consumer could incur.

For the QHP, the coinsurance amounts (numbers depicted in the table as a percentage) apply once the deductible is met and count toward the out-of-pocket maximum cost. Copayments (numbers depicted in the table with a dollar sign) are paid each time a consumer receives a service, are not subject to the deductible, and do not count toward the out-of-pocket maximum cost.

Rehabilitation is provided to help a person regain, maintain or prevent deterioration of a skill that has been acquired but then lost or impaired due to illness, injury, or disabling condition. While federal law does not define habilitative services, habilitation has been defined by several advocacy groups as a service that is provided in order for a person to attain, maintain, or prevent deterioration of a skill or function never learned or acquired due to a disabling condition.

The Patient Protection and Affordable Care Act (PPACA) required that, effective January 1, 2014, states determine Medicaid and CHIP income eligibility for certain categories of individuals using a uniform modified adjusted gross income (MAGI) methodology that is derived from a federal tax based definition of income. To accomplish this, states were required to convert their net income eligibility standards to MAGI equivalent income standards. The CHIP eligibility FPL ranges in this table reflect this conversion. Additionally, PPACA specifies that an income disregard equal to five percentage points of the FPL be deducted from an individual's income when determining Medicaid and CHIP eligibility. The FPL eligibility ranges in this table do not reflect this income disregard.

[a]Copayment paid after deductible met.

[b]If generic prescription drugs are ordered through the mail, the cost per prescription is $20 and is subject to the prescription deductible.

[c]If brand-name prescription drugs are ordered through the mail, the cost per prescription is $40 and is subject to the prescription deductible. Brand- name drugs include drugs designated by the plan as "preferred" or included in their formulary.

[d]This coinsurance is not subject to the deductible. [e]Not covered unless following a cochlear implant.

[f] Routine transportation includes transportation to and from medical appointments.

End Notes

[1] Medicaid is a joint federal-state program that finances health insurance coverage for certain categories of lower-income individuals, including children. Most states' upper income CHIP eligibility levels are between 200 and 300 percent of the federal poverty level (FPL), with the highest eligibility level being 400 percent of the FPL.

[2] Pub. L. No. 111-148, 124 Stat. 119 (2010). In this report, references to PPACA include any amendments made by the Health Care and Education Reconciliation Act of 2010, Pub. L. No. 111-152, 124 Stat. 1029 (2010), unless otherwise indicated. PPACA required the establishment of health insurance exchanges in each state by January 1, 2014, to allow consumers to compare participating individual health insurance plans, known as QHPs and SADPs, available in that state and enroll in coverage. In states electing not to operate their own exchange, PPACA requires the federal government to establish and operate an exchange in the state, referred to as a federally facilitated exchange. QHPs and SADPs offered in the exchanges must meet certain minimum requirements, including those relating to coverage and cost. The Department of Health and Human Services' Centers for Medicare & Medicaid Services (CMS), which is tasked with overseeing the establishment of exchanges, refers to exchanges as marketplaces.

[3] The Secretary is required to report by April 2015 on comparability of benefits and cost sharing between CHIP and QHPs. As of January 2015, CMS had not issued guidance on how comparability between QHPs and CHIP will be defined. Given the uncertainty regarding the affordability and adequacy of children's coverage outside of CHIP, the Medicaid and CHIP Payment and Access Commission recommended that Congress extend federal CHIP funding for a transition period of 2 years. CHIP regulations also generally require that, for children found ineligible for CHIP, either at the time of initial application or during a follow-up eligibility determination, the state must screen the child for Medicaid eligibility and, if ineligible for Medicaid, the state must then screen for potential eligibility for other insurance affordability programs, including subsidized coverage in a QHP.

[4] As of January 2015, 42 states operated separate CHIP programs (1 state had a separate CHIP program only and 41 states covered CHIP children through both a separate CHIP program and Medicaid.) The number of states that cover CHIP children through both a separate CHIP program and Medicaid increased in 2014 due to federal requirements in PPACA that children ages 6 to18 in families earning under 133 percent FPL must be covered under Medicaid.

[5] To prepare for the offering of QHPs in 2014, HHS asked states to select benchmark health plans—plans intended as models for the benefits that would be offered through QHPs. Benchmark plans were not models for QHP cost-sharing. Instead, PPACA includes provisions that standardize QHP costs and reduce cost-sharing for certain individuals. GAO, *Children's Health Insurance: Information on Coverage of Services, Costs to Consumers, and Access to Care in CHIP and Other Sources of Insurance*, GAO-14-40 (Washington, D.C.: November 21, 2013).

[6] Based on our review of federal regulation and health plan documents, we identified sub-categories of services for further review. We reviewed the following services: ambulatory patient services (primary care physician and specialist office visits and outpatient surgery); emergency care; inpatient hospital services (facility, professional, and ancillary); maternity care; mental health services (inpatient and outpatient); substance abuse services (inpatient and outpatient); prescription drugs; preventive care (well-child care, immunizations, and chronic disease management); outpatient therapies (physical, speech, and occupational

therapies for rehabilitation and habilitation); pediatric dental services (routine, emergency, and other); pediatric vision services (exams and corrective lenses); laboratory services (inpatient and outpatient); pediatric hearing services (testing and hearing aids); durable medical equipment; hospice; and home- and community-based health care.

[7] We limited our review to the following enabling services: office translation services; non-hospice respite care; routine transportation; and care coordination/case management.

[8] These five states cover children through separate CHIP programs and Medicaid; however, for our review, we only examined their separate CHIP programs.

[9] QHPs must offer coverage that meets one of four metal tier levels—bronze, silver, gold, and platinum—that correspond to plans' actuarial value. We focused our review on silver level plans because reduced cost-sharing is available for eligible individuals enrolled in these plans. Sixty-five percent of QHP enrollees in the 36 federally facilitated exchange states chose a silver-level plan in 2014, according to an Assistant Secretary for Planning and Evaluation (ASPE) enrollment report. See the Department of Health and Human Services, *Health Insurance Marketplace: Summary Enrollment Report for the Initial Annual Open Enrollment Period*, Assistant Secretary for Planning and Evaluation Issue Brief (Washington, D.C.: May 1, 2014).

[10] An Evidence of Coverage document is a comprehensive guide to an enrollee's health care coverage. It explains the benefits and cost-sharing; conditions and limitations of coverage; and plan rules. Our analysis did not include other coverage limits, such as unspecified limits based on medical necessity, expected improvement deadlines (e.g., improvement must be expected within 2 months), and drug day limits (e.g., prescriptions filled for 30 days at a time).

[11] ASPE provided data for the following states: Alabama, Alaska, Arizona, Arkansas, Delaware, Florida, Georgia, Idaho, Illinois, Indiana, Iowa, Kansas, Louisiana, Maine, Michigan, Mississippi, Missouri, Montana, Nebraska, New Hampshire, New Mexico, North Carolina, North Dakota, Ohio, Oklahoma, Pennsylvania, South Carolina, Tennessee, Texas, Utah, Virginia, West Virginia Wisconsin, and Wyoming. We did not obtain similar enrollment data from states using their own state-based exchanges.

[12] EPSDT services include comprehensive screenings, preventive health care services, and other services necessary to correct illnesses or conditions identified by the screenings.

[13] This annual cumulative maximum applies to premiums, deductibles and any applicable cost-sharing requirements, including copayments and coinsurance, irrespective of the number of children in the family who are enrolled in CHIP.

[14] In 2014, Kentucky, Nevada, and Washington required children obtaining coverage in their state-based exchanges to enroll in an SADP if their QHP did not include the pediatric dental benefit.

[15] Deductibles, co-pays, coinsurance amounts, and out-of-pocket maximum costs can vary within these plans, as long as the overall cost-sharing structure meets the required AV levels. Plans are allowed a de minimis variation of +/- 2 percent. Premium costs are not included in the AV computation.

[16] Plans are allowed a de minimis variation of +/- 1 percent.

[17] Each state can divide up areas of residence in the state into locations called rating areas, and issuers of QHPs may vary premiums based on rating area.

[18] If an individual who is eligible for premium tax credits enrolls in a QHP and an SADP, the portion of the SADP that is allocable to the pediatric dental EHB must be considered part of the QHP premium to which the individual's premium tax credit applies. However, unless the consumer purchases a QHP with a premium that is less than the second lowest cost

silver plan, e.g., a bronze plan, the consumer would likely pay the full premium for the SADP.

[19] This applies only to children enrolled in a separate CHIP plan. In the event of a CHIP funding shortfall, children enrolled in a CHIP-funded Medicaid expansion would remain eligible for Medicaid, at least until fiscal year 2019, during which time states may not reduce Medicaid eligibility levels for children. Children remaining Medicaid eligible would not qualify for premium tax credits or cost-sharing subsidies.

[20] 77 Fed. Reg. 73118, 73165 (Dec. 7, 2012) (codified at 45 C.F.R. § 155.305(g)(3)). According to CMS, the agency adopted this rule because it would be operationally difficult for an issuer to establish separate cost-sharing amounts for different enrollees covered under the same policy.

[21] Officials from each of the selected states reported that they had not undertaken efforts to compare CHIP and QHP coverage and costs.

[22] Additionally, habilitative services were not covered by the selected CHIP plan in Kansas.

[23] Selected CHIP plans and QHPs were similar in that most did not cover non-hospice respite care.

[24] We refer to pediatric dental services as those other than non-emergency dental only. Officials from two large national issuer associations noted several factors that may have contributed to their QHP issuers' decisions not to include coverage for pediatric dental services in 2014, including lack of experience offering these services, concerns about how the additional cost of providing these services could affect their competitiveness, and the option to not provide them if an SADP was available in the state. QHP offerings may be different in 2015, however. According to Colorado officials, more QHPs in their state have included pediatric dental services in 2015 than did in 2014 primarily because of administrative simplification. Additionally, plan officials for the Utah SADP told us the selected SADP would be discontinued at the end of 2014, as the dental benefits offered would be embedded in the issuer's medical plans in 2015.

[25] Each state's CHIP was the model for dental benefits in Colorado, Illinois, Kansas, and New York QHPs and SADPs in 2014. Utah's benchmark plan was the model for dental benefits in Utah's QHPs and SADPs.

[26] According to CMS, a QHP must offer check-ups, basic, and major dental services to be considered a QHP with embedded dental coverage. According to our analysis of enrollment data for 2014 provided by ASPE, less than half of the QHPs in a given state offered any type of dental coverage—checkups, basic, or major dental services—in two thirds of states with federally facilitated exchanges.

[27] See Department of Health and Human Services, *Health Insurance Marketplace: Summary Enrollment Report.*

[28] Utah is the only selected state that imposed a deductible on its CHIP population. In 2014, CHIP enrollees in Utah with family incomes between 134 and 150 percent FPL were subject to a deductible of $40 a year for the family. Those with family incomes between 151 and 200 percent FPL were subject to an annual deductible of $500 and $1,500 for a child and family, respectively.

[29] These annual deductible amounts were for the 94 percent AV plan. To qualify for the 94 percent AV plan, enrollees must have family incomes at or below 150 percent FPL. The deductibles for the lower AV plans (70, 73, and 87 percent) were often considerably higher. See appendix IV.

[30] A copayment is a fixed dollar amount that a consumer must pay at the time a covered service is provided. Coinsurance is a fixed percentage of the total cost of covered services that a consumer must pay.

[31] The selected CHIP plan in Utah differed from the selected CHIP plans in the other four states in that that it imposed either a copayment or coinsurance on nearly all services we reviewed, which varied by income level.

[32] According to the Health Care Cost Institute, the average price of an inpatient stay, which includes hospital stays, in 2011 was $15,674. See the Health Care Cost Institute, *Health Care Cost and Utilization Report: 2011* (Washington, D.C., Health Care Cost Institute, 2012).

[33] The lowest income enrollees fall in the lowest FPL range that CHIP covers in each respective state. This range was between 143 and 156 percent for Colorado, greater than 142 and up to 157 percent for Illinois, between 134 and 166 percent for Kansas, greater than 154 and less than 160 percent for New York, and between 134 and 150 percent FPL for Utah.

[34] In some cases, enrolling previously eligible CHIP children into QHPs could reduce premium costs for families. This is because CHIP plans and QHPs each have statutory limits on premiums based on family income, and the limits applied to each program do not account for families that pay premiums to both programs, known as premium stacking. More than 3 million children are subject to CHIP premiums, so many families enrolling in exchanges may be subject to premium stacking if they also purchase CHIP plans. In contrast, some families with CHIP-eligible children may not qualify for premium tax credits and, therefore, enrolling previously eligible CHIP children into QHPs could increase their premium costs. Specifically, families do not qualify for QHP subsidies if a parent is offered "affordable" employer coverage. The law considers employer coverage affordable if the cost of the employee-only plan—without the cost of additional family members—does not exceed 9.5 percent of household income. This is often referred to as the "family glitch," as the actual premium that a family pays for insurance may be much higher than 9.5 percent. See GAO, *Children's Health Insurance: Opportunities Exist for Improved Access to Affordable Insurance,* GAO-12-648 (Washington, D.C.: June 22, 2012).

[35] If an individual who is eligible for premium tax credits enrolls in a QHP and an SADP, the portion of the SADP that is allocable to the pediatric dental EHB must be considered part of the QHP premium to which the individual's premium tax credit applies. However, unless the consumer purchases a QHP with a premium that is less than the second lowest cost silver plan, e.g., a bronze plan, the consumer would likely pay the full premium for the SADP.

[36] PPACA out-of-pocket maximum costs on EHB for households with incomes between 100 and 400 percent of the FPL in 2014 ranged from $2,250 to $6,350 for individuals and $4,500 to $12,700 for families. In 2015, out-of-pocket maximum costs on EHB for households with incomes between 100 and 400 percent of the FPL ranged from $2,250 to $6,600 for individuals and from $4,500 to $13,200 for families.

[37] Similarly, a recent report by Avalere Health found that 74 percent of silver level QHPs in 2015 have out-of-pocket maximum costs that are below PPACA-established limits. Avalere Health LLC, *Consumers Should Look at Maximum Out-of-Pocket Limits & Deductibles in the Exchanges* (Washington, D.C., Avalere Health LLC, 2014).

[38] The selected SADP in Utah differed from the selected SADPs in the other three states in that it imposed an out-of-pocket maximum cost of $40 for the low plan and $20 for the high plan. CMS regulations impose uniform out-of-pocket maximum costs on SADPs beginning in

2015. Under these regulations, cost-sharing may not exceed $350 for one covered child and $700 for two or more covered children.

End Note for Appendix III

[1]For the QHP in New York, cost-sharing amounts reflect PPACA-established subsidies that are available to certain enrollees through lower out-of-pocket maximum costs and, if necessary, through lower deductibles, copayments, or coinsurance. Once the adjustments from the subsidies are made, the actuarial value of the plan effectively increases from 70 percent to 73, 87, or 94 percent, depending on income.

End Note for Appendix IV

[1] The plan variations reflect the PPACA-established cost-sharing subsidies through lower out-of-pocket maximum costs and, if necessary, through lower deductibles, copayments, or coinsurance. Once the adjustments from the subsidies are made, the actuarial values effectively increase from 70 percent to 73, 87, or 94 percent, depending on income.

INDEX

I

L

M

N

O

U

V

W

X

Z